Behind Every Good Man

Candid thoughts for preachers' wives and those who love them

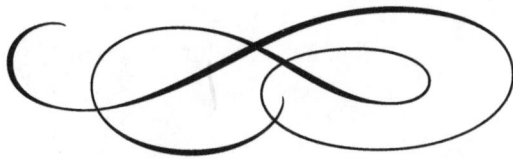

Published by
Spiritbuilding Publishing
15591 N. State Rd. 9, Summitville, IN 46070

Printed in the United States of America

Jamerson, Joyce
Behind Every Good Man
ISBN 9780982981122

Spiritbuilding
Publishing

Spiritual "equipment" for the contest of life.

The Preacher's Wife[1]

—Miriam M. Morrison—

You may think it quite an easy task,
And just a pleasant life;
But really it takes a lot of grace
To be a preacher's wife.
She's supposed to be a paragon
Without a fault in view,
A saint when in the parsonage
As well as in the pew.

Her home must be a small hotel
For folks that chance to roam,
And yet have peace and harmony
The perfect preacher's home.
Whenever groups are called to meet
Her presence must be there,
And yet the members all agree
She should live a life of prayer.

Though hearing people's burdens,
Their grief both night and day,
She's supposed to spread but sunshine
To those along the way.
She must lend a sympathetic ear
To every tale of woe
And then forget it,
Lest it to others go.

Her children must be models rare
Of quietness and poise,
But still stay on the level
With other girls and boys.
You may think it quite an easy task,
And just a pleasant life,
But really it takes a lot of grace
To be a preacher's wife.

---

[1] http://www.ministrymagazine.org/archives/1961/MIN1961–09.pdf

Acknowledgements

From the birth of the idea, to the completion of this work, many hands were involved. Thank you first of all, to these good women who gave of their time to research, study and write, all while dealing with the daily pressures of life. Two of these brave souls were even in the process of relocating! They believed this book was needed and their willingness and cooperation have been a blessing and encouragement to me.

A special thank you to two exceptional proof readers: First, my faithful friend, Katie Mitchell, who continues to objectively lend her talents to help an old woman who still needs to refresh long-forgotten rules of grammar and to my dear husband, who not only helps to proof the material, but continues his loving support for any of my writing adventures. Amanda Burnett willingly offered her talents for the cover photo. Thank you all.

Finally, I thank God for presenting this opportunity. It is my prayer that this will be a work that will bring encouragement to sisters in Christ, help to develop deeper commitment and as a result, bring glory and honor to His name.

Table of Contents

Introduction
by Joyce Jamerson

After our companion book *Behind the Preacher's Door* was released, many comments were received about how much a similar book is needed for preachers' *wives*. It has been both a challenge and a joy to see this book come together. There are no manuals, no *how to* books, or sets of directions for being a preacher's wife. Even in Scripture, there are no special references or directions to preachers' wives, above that given to all women. Scripture is still our guide; a complete guide through the ages—in changing times. We see changes in this generation—lack of respect is now common; not only for authority but for one another. It's known as the **me** generation and it filters into the church. We could more appropriately call this selfishness a lack of love; failure to develop in the fruit of the Spirit. Do these things translate into our daily lives? You be the judge. In preparation for this book, seven questions were distributed to a group of women by e-mail, including but not limited to preachers' wives. Two of the questions were for everyone, the remaining five only for preachers' wives. I'll refer more to that later, but consider this question, addressed only to preachers' wives:

I see this changing trend among preachers' wives _____.

The answers were revealing. Maybe we're more influenced by changing times than we thought?

Changing Trends

- ♦ More talk and less action.
- ♦ Unwilling to be in front and lead women in Scripture or use their talents to write women's Bible class material.
- ♦ More career-oriented than being a helpmeet to their husbands.
- ♦ More work outside the home.

- ◆ Materialism.
- ◆ Unwilling to be hospitable to anyone.
- ◆ Not taking part.
- ◆ Expects husband to carry her work load.
- ◆ Not having people in their homes for Bible classes or social gatherings.
- ◆ Having a selfish attitude towards getting involved in husbands work. Some work outside the home and use this as an excuse.
- ◆ More inclined to go along with culture in attitude, dress, working outside the home.
- ◆ Preachers' wives have entered the work force in mass. Unfortunately, it has for many become an absolute necessity for her to supplement her husband's income so the family can simply survive.

Paul's words to the saints at Philippi seem to be contemporary to our time. He had an immense joy because of their obedience to Christ, but it was not without concern.

> *Therefore if there is any encouragement in Christ, if there is any consolation of love, if there is any fellowship of the Spirit, if any affection and compassion, make my joy complete by being of the same mind, maintaining the same love, united in spirit, intent on one purpose. Do nothing from selfishness or empty conceit, but with humility of mind regard one another as more important than yourselves; do not merely look out for your own personal interests, but also for the interests of others. Have this attitude in yourselves which was also in Christ Jesus,* Philippians 2:1–5.

Even though they had administered to him in many ways, he still reminded them of their need for humility as they went about their daily lives. God was at work in them and Paul knew the joy they had in serving others. This joy should be shared, even as difficult trials surrounded them. He warned them of potential dangers, challenged them to rejoice, and in doing this, they would find the peace of God.

This book has a similar purpose. Although we see rapid change as time goes on, we still find joy to share among difficult trials, we still administer to one another, and we still have the need for humility. To be warned of potential dangers and challenged concerning the future is sorely needed, both when we tend to forget our goals and when the goal seems unobtainable. Philippians is very much a book for preachers' wives. Its applications are striking when read with that view.

Pressure, rather than spiritual growth, can control our actions.

In these changing times, we want to conduct ourselves in a manner worthy of the gospel of Christ; we want our reputation to be one of standing firm. As Paul had to be separated from Timothy, his kindred spirit, we have to be separated as well, from those we have loved and taught. Sin has to be dealt with and those who have been led astray rescued, all the while living among brethren who have differing opinions and ideas. We must press on and rejoice while doing it, training our minds to think on things that are *"true, honorable, right, pure, lovely and of good repute,"* Philippians 4:8, NASV.

It's a lofty task. Not all of us do it well. Pressure, rather than spiritual growth, can control our actions. Because of our actions, others can be discouraged and some husbands have had to relocate much more often than they would otherwise, because of their wives' inability to exercise self-control. There are many areas in which self-control and self-examination is needed. Amid our daily frustrations, can we learn to be content within our circumstances? Can we get along with those who differ in life-style? Can we live humbly or in prosperity? Are we a help or a hindrance to our husbands? Will our actions cause someone else to stumble spiritually? Do we need an attitude adjustment?

Paul had learned the secret, Philippians 4:13. We can too. Good women gave up some of their summertime activity to work on this project; addressing some difficult topics—ones perhaps that we'd rather leave dormant. Because they saw the need, two of our writers stepped out of their comfort zone to put pen to paper for the very first time. What a joy! What a blessing for me to see the work of all these women come together in this form. This book will help us take a good look at the woman behind the good man—the preacher's wife.

An Inside Look
—The Preaching Life—
by Joyce Jamerson

P reaching has long been a curiosity. In the minds of many, preachers are on a pedestal. As a girl, I remember great excitement when
we were getting a new preacher, and I was particularly curious
about his family. How old were they? Did they have children? I'm sure
everyone wanted them to be close to their age. Getting a new preacher
didn't happen very often, so with the arrival came great anticipation.
Care was taken to welcome them, often filling their pantry or having a
special party so they could get to know everyone. My parents were usually close to the preacher and his family, for my dad served as an elder.
We were challenged and uplifted by them and profited by their good
influence. The preacher was very capable and the preacher's wife was
pleasant, kind, and happy. She had great influence on me and I would
often baby-sit their well behaved children. It saddened me greatly when
I saw her crying one day, explaining to my mom how someone had hurt
her feelings. A catty comment was made about the dress she was wearing.
With that event (plus others like it) tucked back in my memory, I met
and married a preacher.

As a girl, I loved to sit at the table, listening to preacher stories.
During a gospel meeting, my parents would always invite the visiting preacher over on Sunday night to have sandwiches since they both
worked on week days and it would have been difficult to prepare a meal
otherwise. Those simple times were some of the best. People don't often
serve sandwiches anymore, at least the way Mom did. She put everything
on the table and we all made our own. Simple, yes, but Mom found that
her sandwich night was a favorite among many who came our way. Little
did I know that those Sunday night sessions were actually preparing me
to be a preacher's wife. The thought of being such had not entered my

mind until Frank and I met when he came to a congregation across town to do his first full time preaching. There were not many Christians close to my age in our area, so in looking back, we believe that God's providence was at work.

During our dating years, as our relationship was growing, a fellow worker asked me, "What do you *do* on a date with a preacher?" It was a funny question because people of the world think preachers are to be feared and cannot possibly have any fun. It didn't take long to know that people looked at preachers a little differently. On a recent work day at our place of worship, there were things that needed attention; so of course, we all went in our work clothes. (There was painting involved, so we were really scrubby looking.) One young woman made the comment that seeing us in work clothes was blowing her mind; she had a mental picture of always seeing us in *Sunday best.* Contrary to what some must think, preachers don't stay dressed up all the time and they do not sleep in their ties!

Since there are no manuals or crash courses on how to be a preacher's wife, I hoped for the best and asked advice from others whom I admired. Curiously, I wonder what the statistics would be if we took a poll of preachers' wives. Everyone has a story. Did they know that's what they wanted? Did it just happen that the man they met and married was a preacher? Or did his decision to preach come after the wedding? In any event, hearts that truly love God will be successful, Luke 10:27; Psalm 31:23–24. If you are a preacher's wife, you have chosen to be by his side, and your help, your encouragement, your positive outlook, will sustain him through good times and bad. Preachers' wives are no different in that aspect than any other wife. We want our husbands to be successful in life and in their chosen vocations, but being in the public eye will deliver a twist to the responsibilities of a preacher's wife.

Questions in the poll (mentioned in the introduction) are as follows; the first two addressed to all who participated; the rest only to preachers' wives:

- What are the top 5 things you would like to see in a preacher's wife?
- What are the top 5 things about preacher's wives that disappoint you?

If you are a preacher's wife, finish these sentences:

- Brethren have no right to: _____
- The best thing about being a PW is: _____
- The hardest thing about being a PW is: _____
- I see this changing trend among preachers' wives: _____
- The funniest thing that happened to us was:_____

Again, the results were very interesting. In this chapter we'll investigate two more questions, and later in the book the results to the remaining questions will be revealed.

Top Five Things You Like to See in a Preacher's Wife

Friendly was the number one answer, with **hospitable** following second with one notation that they should be *cheerfully* hospitable. Other submissions will be listed in groups, as follows:

Spiritual Concerns

- Serious Bible student
- Knowledgeable
- Ability to teach women
- Spiritual leadership and Bible knowledge
- Spiritually minded and committed to God's truth

- Willing to attend & teach ladies Bible classes
- Dedication to Bible studies (Some do not attend extra studies but always have time for kids activities or card groups.)
- Excited to teach children's classes
- Concern for the church
- Deep awareness of life's brevity

Personal Qualities

- Trustworthy
- Honest
- Love
- Genuine Concern
- Loyalty
- Compassion
- Kindness
- Gracious
- Cheerful
- Down to earth
- Calming; quiet leader – not pushy or domineering
- Humility
- Generosity of spirit
- Sense of humor
- Easily approachable
- Personable
- I like to see her smile – she must be exhausted
- Keeps things in perspective
- Discretion
- Modesty
- An obviously healthy marriage; others need to see how godly couples deal with struggles, enjoy each other and work to improve their marriage

♦ Don't think of yourself as a preacher's wife – but a Christian woman who happens to be married to a preacher; a distinct person with your own unique abilities, talents, and needs

Relating to Others

♦ Keeps secrets and confidences — a safe place for others to share problems
♦ Encourages others
♦ Slow to criticize
♦ Right words for right occasion
♦ Willingness to befriend all females in congregation
♦ Creating ways and means for others to do good deeds
♦ Not partial or inclusive
♦ Show hospitality without partiality
♦ Accepting disposition
♦ Devoted to husband and family
♦ Have obedient children that show respect to others
♦ True help meet; subjection to husband
♦ 100% behind husband
♦ Truly loves brethren
♦ Ability to counsel younger women soundly with compassion and love and do it well
♦ The best preachers and wives are part of a team.

If I had been presented such a list when I was newly married, I think I would have fainted!

On the lighter side—*a preacher's wife must be:*

♦ Exciting yet calm
♦ Lovely yet plain
♦ Stylish but conservative in dress
♦ Greets everyone enthusiastically yet stays in the background
♦ A good conversationalist but never loud

- ◆ Up to date on current events but never opinionated
- ◆ Good homemaker, with office experience
- ◆ Young but wise; with 30 years of experience
- ◆ Cheerful yet contemplative
- ◆ Can critique without finding fault
- ◆ Generous but frugal
- ◆ Good organizer but never gives orders
- ◆ Experienced counselor yet never gives advice
- ◆ Old school yet innovative

Ready for the Challenge?

From Scripture, we form our own guidelines of what God expects of women and what we should be as preachers' wives. Then we form another set of what the congregation expects of us, and it can change from place to place. It has been correctly stated that God is the only one we have to please, but on the other hand, that's not an excuse for failing to develop some people skills. Know your strengths and your weaknesses and focus on those strengths. Preachers are not all alike and neither are their wives. All will vary in personality and strengths and some have to work harder than others to be a people person; *others centered* instead of *self-centered*. With practice, it will become part of life. Love, kindness, goodness, and gentleness are the fruit of the Spirit, (as well as doing it with joy and striving for peace) and every Christian woman should work on these qualities. Let's throw faithfulness and self-control in there too, so we can work on all nine! Our lives reflect our growth or lack of it as a Christian, and have very little to do with being married to a preacher.

College classes gave me some preparation, especially Bible classes, but I felt woefully unprepared to be a preacher's wife. Being in love, knowing how to cook, and how to be friendly helped me to survive—plus being encouraged by wonderful brothers and sisters around me, who were readily anxious to help a young preacher and his wife.

Congregations then didn't have the teaching programs that so many have today. Team teaching would have been an immense help. Having a mentor and learning from a seasoned teacher would have been a wonderful support but women of that time were reluctant to share their ideas, and heaven forbid that anyone should witness them teaching a class! Very quickly after our marriage, I was expected to be involved in the teaching process (never having been encouraged to teach at my home congregation) so the students and I learned together! (Being involved in an organized teaching program is extremely beneficial, not only for the congregation but for the preacher's wife as well. My first experience with organizing one quickly revealed my flaws, but it was the best learning experience I've ever had.)

Fortunately we were across town from my parents, and I had a little time to adapt to my new challenges before having to leave them and my hometown. Moving has to be one of the greatest challenges. It can be a strain for all the family, but getting to know people from different regions has been an exciting and unique blessing for us and for our children. There are good things to be said about staying a long time in one location, and other good things can be said about change. Either way, it's a challenge, but living in different locales is an education in itself as is getting to know and being able to work with different personalities. I was excited but apprehensive as we left Richmond. Surely, I would need to be *perfect* and if I could only keep hidden all my insecurities and my lack of Bible knowledge, maybe we could get by. Already familiar with criticism, I could no longer rely on my parents for advice, and in spite of having a wonderful husband and a four month old baby, I felt very alone. Personal growth is slow and steady. No one has come up with an instant formula. Experiences in the years that followed taught me that some are anxious and willing to help and some are more willing to criticize. I will be held accountable for my actions; they for their judgments.

The second question of the poll:

The Top Five Things That Disappoint You in Preachers' Wives

This list is varied as well. Hospitality was seen as important, and in this poll, lack of hospitality was most mentioned, tying for second was gossip and a holier than thou attitude.

Spiritual Concerns

- Gossip
- Holier than thou attitude
- Neglects teaching Bible classes ~ both women and children
- There's not a point in which we should retire!
- Unwilling to teach women's classes
- Prevents husband from overseas work
- Does not lead with loving example
- Isn't honest about having troubles of her own
- Fails to realize others look to her for leadership

Personal Qualities

- Haughty
- Overbearing
- Has noticeable favorites; cliquish
- Rude
- Judgmental
- Distant
- No personality
- Unapproachable; standoffish
- Unfriendly
- Worldly
- Materialistic
- Selfish
- Complainer
- Doesn't try to live within means

♦ Lack of self-control, especially with tongue
♦ More tied to parents than husband
♦ Doesn't support husband and speaks negatively of him
♦ Interrupts husband too often at office
♦ Takes authority they don't have
♦ Lets others spoil their children
♦ Children not in control
♦ Makes excuses for kids because they're preacher's kids
♦ Not discreet in their dress as an example to others
♦ Attire and Modesty — please, sew up the slit in those skirts!

Relating to Others

♦ Lack of hospitality
♦ Attentive to a chosen few
♦ Not involved in well-being of members
♦ Not making time for others
♦ Never has members over to get to know them
♦ Doesn't interact with members
♦ Lack of personal contact
♦ Don't even know her — is she shy?
♦ Being in a clique and not giving attention to others equally
♦ Stays out of public eye
♦ Criticizes brethren
♦ Inability to connect to all ages
♦ Doesn't call members when absent
♦ Expects things to be given to her
♦ Not interested in Christian sisters outside of worship
♦ Lack of understanding about keeping private matters private
♦ Not in control of their tongue; unable to handle confidential matters

It was very interesting to see how others view the work of a preacher's wife — including preachers' wives! But the most appreciated comment by this editor:

> *Preachers' wives do their best under very trying*
> *circumstances. I expect nothing more from the preacher's*
> *wife than from Christian women anywhere.*

Contemplating these lists brings varied reactions. First, we may think, "How could I possibly be all these things? How can I possibly be all things to all people?" **All** women, whether they have husbands or not and whether husbands preach or serve in some other capacity, should be striving to fulfill the qualities on these lists. What positive changes could you imagine seeing in the Lord's church if **everyone** practiced developing these qualities?

> *Put on a heart of compassion, kindness, humility,*
> *gentleness and patience; bearing with one another, and*
> *forgiving one another,* Colossians 3:12.

> *Pray for us, for we are sure that we have a good*
> *conscience, desiring to conduct ourselves honorably in all*
> *things,* Hebrews 13:18.

My husband teases me by saying my foreign mission work began when we moved to the south. It was my first Deep South experience, where hog's heads were in the grocery meat cases and recipes for crackling bread were frequently shared. Moving from a large city to a small southern town took more courage than I knew I had.

Even though I didn't know it then, experiences on my grandparent's farm as a kid were good preparation. Both my brother and I milked cows and worked in the garden, and this taste of country life enabled me to appreciate the lifestyle and work ethics of some country folks. We have been privileged to share meals in elaborate houses (where the table was carefully set and the meal was served in courses) as well as farm houses (where there was no air conditioning and the breeze through the window told us there was a pig pen a few yards away) and the meal was served from pots on the stove. And you know what? Each host loved the Lord and wanted to do His will, while sharing with others.

Customs vary all over the United States, and certainly in other nations. What we take for granted in our area may actually be offensive in other areas! (For instance, saying Yes Ma'am and No Sir. In the south, children are trained to politely answer in this way; and in some areas, especially the north, some are offended and ask not to be called Ma'am.) Being flexible, asking a lot of questions, and observing before speaking are good traits to develop that can help to avoid some very embarrassing moments.

Preaching itself presents unique opportunities and growth occurs as these are experienced. If I had known some of the challenges that would be presented ahead of time, I would have thought, *No way!* But step by step, the challenges were met and conquered. Isn't that how any growth takes place? We may be fearful about some situations, but with prayer and a steady helper by our side, we find them doable. Even though Timothy was young, Paul tells him to be an example to those who believe in these areas: speech, conduct, love, faith, and purity, 1 Timothy 4:12. All Christians need to be that type of example; here again, it is not unique to either the preacher or

> *We can make or break our husbands' influence just by our actions, our dress or our involvement.*

his wife. It takes time and effort to grow in these areas. Preachers' wives are behind-the-scenes workers. *(Many times I've said preachers' wives are anonymous if not seen with their husbands!)* There are no awards for best supporting preacher's wife; in fact, many things done may go without notice. That's all right; the only award we really care about is the one received on the last great day.

It can be easy to let pride creep in when introduced as the preacher's wife, or when complimented about Bible teaching skills. Our place in the Kingdom is no more important than any other, our prayers do not go any higher, and we do not have a special pipeline to God. We're working together to reach a common goal. In fact, most preachers' wives that I know *prefer* to be just one of the gang with no special treatment. Being introduced as the preacher's wife can sometimes be used as a warning to others to be careful of how they act or what they say, since there is a *religious* person present. On the other hand, being introduced as the preacher's wife may open up conversation that would not have taken place otherwise. Even though our husbands are our spiritual leaders and their relationship with God directly affects us, it is easy to fall into the trap of thinking we can ride into heaven on our husband's coattails. Even though we do everything possible to let him be free to do his work, there are plenty of days when we're exhausted with the cares of the day. Permitting daily urgencies to crowd out the important will help us lose touch with our own spiritual needs and growth. No amount of helping others can take the place of our spiritual development.

Whether we want to be or not, we *are* in a place of leadership and influence and need to be conscious of our appearance when we are with others. Most women, but especially young girls, see the preacher's wife as a role model. Soon after Frank and I married, this realization hit me with force and it's never been forgotten. A young girl, probably twelve or thirteen at the time, asked her mother to buy the same kind of shampoo that she had seen in my bathroom. Shampoo leadership strikes us as being funny, but in what *other* areas would she be watching? Influence can be strong or wrong.

There are several admonitions to women—*all* women—in Scripture concerning their behavior; our behavior as preachers' wives is just a little more noticeable. Some refer to it as a *fishbowl* or *glass house* existence, but being conscious of influence can work to make us better. What will become of those who turn away because they were discouraged with our example? Adjusting some of our habits is a small sacrifice when compared to the sacrifices others before us have made.

Some critique and criticize, but please note: Those who are active and busy have very little time to critique. Realize though, that we can make or break our husbands' influence just by our actions, our dress, or our involvement. Help or hindrance? We choose. Even though many of us have the convenience of owning two cars, which means that waiting through lengthy business meetings is no longer a problem, we still have to guard against leaving our husbands to do everything alone. Even those who have been married many years need to protect their relationship and their marriage! It is noticed when a couple never sits together or always comes to worship in separate cars. Our men need to know that we love them and love what they're doing. Because of the needs of children, health difficulties, and other family concerns, there will be times when we cannot be with our husbands, but our interest should always be in their work and their effectiveness in God's kingdom.

There are disadvantages to any line of work. You may have to rescue your husband at some point, by reminding him that his family comes first. When so many others would like a piece of his time, family time almost has to be scheduled. Long ago, Frank was extremely busy with many new prospects. He was gone almost every night, involved in home studies, and when he wasn't teaching, he was studying. Even though we have a duty to teach the lost, our primary duty is to establish a home that honors God, and to raise children who will glorify Him. One evening I plainly told him, "I do not intend to sit here and let you ignore us." Many preachers become so involved in ministering to others; their children become discouraged and bitter because they don't have a dad, and wives struggle with resentment because of the burdens placed upon them.

All disadvantages are firmly outweighed by rich experiences! Where else could you be with the best people in the world, eat at the tables of the best cooks in the world, enjoy association with so many dedicated Christians and get paid for it?

Preachers and their families are usually full of interesting stories, and there are many life stories to tell; some you couldn't make up if you tried! Start a journal (see Becky Allen's chapter on Homemaking), and in years to come, your family will enjoy remembering stories from the past.

Where do we begin when we want to put a puzzle together? First, look at the overall picture; then fill in the edges. There's not a preacher's wife living who knew the complete picture and all the right things to do from the very beginning. Each will grow in wisdom as growth in Christ takes place. If not, what would be the point of Peter's admonition in 2 Peter 1? We are to diligently *add* to our faith with virtue, knowledge, self-control, perseverance, godliness, brotherly kindness, and love, NKJV.

So get ready. We'll journey more of that road together as you continue reading this special collection of articles written by dedicated preachers' wives.

1 Corinthians 13 for Preachers' Wives
—{A Paraphrase}—

If I am happy, outgoing and well-behaved and please all the sisters with my ability to get things done, but have not love, life is empty and means nothing. If I'm on time for everything, handle phone calls like a secretary, stay in touch through Facebook, and respond promptly to every e-mail; if I have a clean house, serve great meals, and have lots of company, but do not love and guide my children, then none of it matters, and I am nothing.

If I organize the resource room, have a Bible study with friends, or write a book that reaps a few good things in my lifetime, but do not teach my children, then I missed the greatest opportunity in my life and gain nothing.

Love is patient; love is kind. It does not wish troubled members would disappear when they are experiencing difficulty or that their congregation was like someone else's or take personal credit when everything is going well. Love is not arrogant or snobby; it is courteous, even to those kind and polite souls who keep secret some of your less than perfect behavior. It does not hold the visiting preacher meal list or the to-do list above the people they were meant to serve. It does not walk around like a cranky martyr for staying late and having to lock the building, take a second turn at teaching even though you taught last quarter, or any other things one gives up for the overall good of a church family. It does not react in anger or feel a sense of self-pity, but rejoices when truth is taught to everyone who hears and God's Word is honored and glorified. Love holds up under the constant fish bowl existence, it gives its fellow workers the benefit of the doubt; it has great vision for the future and works to that end, patiently enduring the faults of others. Every time we study faith, hope and love, depend on all three, but the greatest of these things is love. Love delights in truth and will never let us down.

Adapted from a blog post by Kristie Braselton (1 Corinthians 13 for Moms)

Just How Faithful are We?
To God—Husband—All Things
by Joanne Beckley

Long ago a woman of Africa came to me with a request, "I have been reading (the Bible) that I must be faithful to my husband. Please teach me how this must be done." Truly we live in a world that does not understand faithfulness, whether toward the God of heaven or toward one another. This woman was a part of this world and surrounded by men who were unfaithful toward their wives. She knew only that obedience was forced upon her and upon every woman in her village. How could I explain to her of what she had not seen, that faithfulness toward her husband requires first, a faithfulness toward herself standing before God? And so I began to talk, my Bible open before me.

The wife of a preacher is no different from this African woman in what is required of her; whether toward God, her husband, her children, or the congregation her husband is serving. Let us begin by examining the word *faithful* as used of God who created and continues to maintain all things. By doing so, we will understand and better accept this quality of *faithfulness* which is listed as a fruit of the Spirit, one that we must develop and maintain, Galatians 5:22.

God is Faithful

Therefore know that the LORD your God, He is God,
the faithful God who keeps covenant and mercy for a
thousand generations with those who love Him and keep
His commandments, Deuteronomy 7:9.

God is not man, that he should lie, or a son of man, that
he should repent. Has he said, and will he not do it?

Or has he spoken, and will he not fulfil it?
Numbers 23:19 RSV.

*Nevertheless My loving kindness I will not utterly take
from him, nor allow My faithfulness to fail. My covenant
I will not break, nor alter the word that has gone out of
My lips. Once I have sworn by My holiness; I will not lie to
David,* Psalm 89:33–35 NKJV.

God's faithfulness toward us begins by acting from the very qualities that
are who He is.

♦ Steadfast in affection or allegiance
♦ Firm to keep His promises
♦ Conscientious and bound by those promises
♦ Loyal and staunch for He will not be tempted to betray our trust
♦ Constant, whether now or in the distant future
♦ Steadfast and unwavering in His love
♦ Resolute to adhere to His purpose

God is indeed faithful to His promises, and He will keep us by
His power, through faith unto salvation, 1 Peter 1:5.

Faithful to God

With these qualities in mind, we can readily understand and accept that these are the very same qualities that we must determine to have
within us if we are to act in faithfulness toward God, holding fast the con-
fession of our hope (Hebrews 10:23), continuing in the faith (Colossians
1:4), filled with thanksgiving, Colossians 2:6–7. No one can be a follower
of Christ who is not faithful. Otherwise, one is deceitful and vain.

In helping us to understand what it means to be faithful to God,
we also have an example in the New Testament of a woman being unfaithful in a surprising way. Read again the familiar story of Mary and
Martha, Luke 10:38–42. Martha was *distracted with much serving*, even

as Mary kept leaving her to go and listen to Jesus. The Greek word for distracted (*periespato*) literally means "to drag around." This is a vivid metaphor that describes how a woman's duties can keep her from concentrating on Him whom she had already determined to serve. We have all seen women whose faces are tight with anxiety, overly concerned with the cares of this life, crowding out her service to God. Jesus rebuked Martha's sharp words of reproach and stated that she had not chosen the better part. She was not faithful to Jesus or herself.

What qualities or attitudes do we need in order to develop faithfulness toward mankind?

The New Testament is loaded with teachings, examples, prohibitions and warnings about our attitudes toward God and one another. These spiritual instructions should be the basis to help us discipline our minds, developing humility, a modesty of heart. By holding God in the highest esteem, revering Him, worshipping and obeying Him, we will give Him our wholehearted love and trust, Matthew 22:37; Romans 12:1–2. We can surely be thus grounded in faithfulness (steadfast in allegiance, loyal, unwavering in love, firm to keep our promises, etc.) toward our fellow man. Conversely, if we allow our attitude toward God to weaken, all other good attitudes toward mankind will deteriorate.

Faithful to our husbands

Faithfulness to God also requires that a preacher's wife must be faithful toward her husband. Look back again at the list describing God's faithfulness. A wife is to have this *same* faithful attitude and action toward her husband. She will be steadfast in allegiance, loyal, unwavering in love, firm to keep her promises, not only in their personal life, but also toward his work as a preacher, being careful to preserve what he has confided in her. She will understand and accept that her conduct can and will impact his own integrity and usefulness to the congregation and to the Lord.

Just as her husband will be tested by temptations, trials, and tribulations, a faithful wife must accept the same, James 1:12; 1 Timothy 3:10; Revelation 2:10. She will be faithful *in all things* to the Lord and to her husband, 1Timothy 1:12; 3:11. Being a woman living for Christ in this evil world is not easy. Being not only a wife but the faithful wife of a preacher is not easy. Every wife must ask herself, will I; can I rise to the challenge?

Faithfulness must of necessity include purity

Faithfulness demands purity of heart and body. W. E. Vine defines purity (*hagnos*) as: "pure from defilement, not contaminated, thus sanctified, set apart . . . chaste." This purity is "personal and moral by nature. It consists in full and unreserved self-offering to God" *(Theological Dictionary of the New Testament)*.

Titus 2:5 and 1 Peter 3:2 give us God's command to be pure and we would do well to honour God in this requirement. A pure heart requires a clean conscience, a positive attitude, and honesty in our actions. A pure heart brings forth truthful words fitly spoken and good timely deeds. A pure heart will not only acknowledge sin in our hearts and seek repentance, but it will readily offer forgiveness.

Because of the times we live in, we must also seriously consider the subject of sexual purity. Nearly everyone we meet is living with someone, unmarried, or committing adultery with the butcher, the baker, and the candlestick maker. Their end is the way of death, Proverbs 14:12. Let us not fall into the trap of thinking we are immune from such. On the contrary, we can list preachers and/or their wives who have been unfaithful. Let us accept the danger and fight for our marriages. Let us keep the marriage bed undefiled, Hebrews 13:4.

Jerry Jenkins wrote a book *Hedges—Loving Your Marriage Enough to Protect It.* He states very plainly and bluntly that spending time with the opposite sex, in sharing private thoughts, is cheating on your own mate. (This is particularly dangerous in our contacts on the internet.) "Perhaps nothing improper was said or done, but simply investing the emotional energy and time is inappropriate. Both individuals interacting should be aware of the potential danger and recognize infatuation for what it is." Although Mr Jenkins is addressing godly men, he also encourages wives to be aware of their husbands' self-protective hedges and support their efforts to remain pure in mind as well as in body. Wives, what about our own hedges? Have we considered them?

Achieving purity in heart and body will require constant effort in all areas of our lives. We must spend much time in Bible study and prayer so that our meditation will develop a strong commitment to desire God's things. By choosing wholesome surroundings for ourselves and our families we are able to choose our friends wisely. By recognizing danger signs—yes, the same warnings we are handing out to our teenage girls— we can set our own ground rules.

Faithful in service to God and man

There is yet one more attitude that we need to emphasize; that of faithful service. No woman, wife, or mother can be such without serving. A preacher's wife will recognize the need to serve in many areas of her life. Serving in a conscientious, steadfast, and resolute way requires getting down and washing feet. Jason Moore gave the following points in a sermon on the value and necessity of serving, using Jesus' example in John 13:1–17:

- ♦ We cannot choose to serve and be worried about our rights.
- ♦ To provide any good, our service has to be practical
- ♦ The decision to serve cannot rely on someone serving you in return
- ♦ The decision to serve does not wait on others to begin serving
- ♦ The servant will choose to serve alone if necessary
- ♦ The decision to serve cannot expect a certain favourable response from the one served
- ♦ The decision to serve must not be reserved for our friends

♦   The decision to serve means you will look and be treated like a
    servant

The blessings Jesus promised in John 13:17 only come by being a servant.
We preachers' wives have our work cut out for us, offering ourselves as
willing sacrifices to God, Romans 12:1.

A wife must be faithful to her husband by her service to him. It
is the role God created for her, Genesis 2:18; Ephesians 5:22; Titus 2:5.
Although everyone must submit to someone, including Christ, a wife has
a special responsibility which she must not shirk. In her obedience she
thus recognizes and honours her husband's leadership, giving thanks to
God. If she does not willingly do so, she reduces, even negates all her husband's efforts to teach and preach, causing him to be seen as weak and
useless in the kingdom of God.

A word of encouragement. We must not only endure, but continue to be suitable helpers whether our husbands' leadership is wise or
foolish. We cannot automatically replace our role of helper with a leadership role. Even a poor leader will benefit from the wisdom of a woman
who remains within her role. Abigail managed to do this and we can also,
1 Samuel 25.

A faithful preacher's wife also needs to consider her willingness
to help her husband in his goals. Too often we wives get caught up with
our own goals that can, in fact, interfere with helping our husbands
achieve their goals. A possible area of concern might be in allowing our
children to become number one in their needs, whether young or older,
instead of our husband's needs. We might ask ourselves, do we jump for
Dad like we do for little Johnny? Taking young teens to their many extra-
curricular activities can be a problem for there is no time to accompany
your husband. If we fill our minds with secular concerns, including eBay,
Facebook, novel reading, etc., we will not keep our minds focused on
spiritual concerns and therefore prepared mentally to help our husbands.

Also, let us reflect on how a wife's outside job can develop into an all-consuming interest, especially as she *climbs the ladder* of success. The list goes on.

Serving in a foreign land

What about if a preacher's wife finds out that her husband has a strong desire and has prayerfully considered serving God in a foreign land? Leaving her comfort zone can be a challenge. Both husband and wife will need to weigh the decision carefully. Both will need to examine what or whom they are truly serving.

Why do I give this advice? From personal experience. When my husband first suggested we look into working for the Lord in a foreign country, I wanted to balk. Sadly, I thought of myself first, for I was comfortable in our situation. I had to sit down and consider the terrible crying need of men and women who had never heard the saving power of the gospel of Jesus Christ. They were and are seeking truth from faithful, trustworthy men (1 Thessalonians 2:4) who will come to them and help them find their Savior, the One whom they can trust (Romans 15:12).

Trust is a precious guardian to the faith. My husband and I learned early that God is totally worthy of our trust. But how can we convey this trust to others? The obvious answer is to put our Lord and His Word into our hearts so that others will trust us and listen to the gospel. We must live our faith and demonstrate our confidence in the Father who created us. This is hard work! A whole lifetime of work. . . . "*Continue in the faith, grounded and steadfast, and are not moved away from the hope of the gospel which you heard,*" Colossians 1:23. My husband and I are in our twenty-fourth year of living in South Africa and teaching among various peoples in Southern Africa. We have three sons who are now living in the States and raising their own children for the Lord. We are alone now, but continuing what we began so many years ago.

You now know **why** I came with my husband to the continent of Africa—but the burning question always arises—**how** did I manage to do it? Or sometimes, how **could** I? I had to leave the security of a great country. (Yes, America truly is. You should see what else is out there!) I had to leave my *roots*, my comfort zone, my *rights* to a comfortable life. I had to leave my parents – and now, my children and my grandchildren behind. How did I do it? Not by being superwoman, but simply by personal conviction.

Conviction is a funny animal. It is a powerful motivator. A woman will endure hardships of many colors—just to achieve what she is convicted of. I have judged and sentenced myself! And what wonders and joys it has brought me. By mutual agreement, David and I **chose** to go to a foreign country to teach the gospel to the many who do not know what God wants from them. *"If Jesus is with me, I'll go—anywhere...."* We did not plan to remain for such a long time, but the hunger (theirs and ours) continues. Yes, I want my two small feet (that are getting bigger as I get older) to have a share in the beauty of bringing the light and peace of the gospel to the lost.

> *If we allow our attitude toward God to weaken, all other good attitudes toward mankind will deteriorate.*

Besides the joys that come with bringing light to dark hearts and watching the *light bulb* go on, one finds great adventures when walking in a foreign culture. Each day has a flavor that makes one want to get up in the morning just to see what the day will bring. A feast for the eye—a colorful native dress, for the ear—a new bird song! Yes, yes, sometimes it all becomes somewhat overwhelming, and then I seek out my rocking chair to knit or crochet a colorful blanket for the needy, pausing to read and pray, meditating on my blessings.

I may spend my day at the computer, studying, making up lessons, grading Bible correspondence courses (still a powerful teaching tool over here), and of course, answering internet correspondence—what an extraordinary blessing! Or, my day may begin with a bout of shopping to purchase from the butcher, the baker, the candlestick maker; necessities only, for the budget is very tight. I love greeting different people, stopping to ask about their day. I have learned that nearly everyone enjoys talking to someone who cares to stop and listen.

I teach three, sometimes four Bible classes for women and children during the week, but the highlight of the week is always on Sunday. Because we travel some distance between the many small churches, our day is full of negotiating around donkeys, chickens, cattle—and potholes. Some you don't ever want to meet again. Whether we meet under a tree, in an old garage, or in a small nicely built brick building, there will be a single drinking glass or a number of small shot glasses and a plate on a table, the floor swept and homemade songbooks opened to the first song. Two to three. . .or four. . . hours later worship services have ended, the translator is resting, and I am sore from sitting on a bench and must go outside to seek cooler air. The mealies are tall, the outhouse is there, hidden, but I shall give it a wide berth. The children are gay in their play, making sure I smile and wave. The women are anxious that I partake of all they can offer. I am so spoiled. My continual prayer—oh, that what I have to offer be as worthwhile.

I came across an interesting fact written by an American preacher who came to Africa and later wrote the following:

> Long ago "Human brooms" were used by porters travelling single-file in Africa. Shivering young children were pushed ahead of carriers in order to dry off the dew from the tall grass onto their bodies. They were called dew breakers. This was the tribal will, for had they not all been through it? The word "pioneer" is coined from this very

*idea of such a one being a "human broom" or "dew break-
er." (Dew Breakers* by Don Merritt, 1971)

I often have cause to reflect on the *wives* of the early pioneer
preachers in America. Their husbands were determined to spread the
gospel, taking their families ever westward, living in *foreign* lands, separated from family and from what they knew of as civilization—dew
breakers for the future. Was not my lot in life similar to their wives, even
though I had crossed the ocean and they had not? How did they face
their hardships? Were they ever so lonely that it was painful to read a letter from Mother? And after they cried, what did they do then?

How did they keep on keeping on? One step at a time, with
thanksgiving. They were ordinary women who loved the Lord and used
what they had at hand to serve their husbands and their Lord. Truly, the
early pioneer preachers and their families got drenched with the dew that
we might go dry. They became my *dew breakers* and I was more than
happy to go to Africa, armed with the knowledge of their faith and perseverance.

*[Editor's note: For more on pioneer preachers' wives, go to Joanne's page
"Sojourning in Distant Lands" at WWW.OURHOPEONLINE.COM]*

I can't help but reflect on how living in another culture while
teaching/preaching the gospel actually develops and accumulates special abilities and skills. Learning to adapt to new situations successfully
gives us a wider understanding not only of the world and her needs, but
a deeper understanding of New Testament times wherein our Scriptures
were written. We have had to face overwhelming trials and overcome
them, including physical dangers. We are stronger spiritually, for if we
are to survive, we will have to face ourselves, whether we are indeed children of God. Our faith develops our values, which forms our decisions,
and in turn builds our character—a life in Christ.

Home away from home? Maybe—but then all of us are only pilgrims "looking for a city where we'll never die." Yes, my husband and I had weighed the pros and cons of our decision and we went. Today, I am 62 years old and I look for young families to come and assist, knowing our productive days are dwindling and the terrible crying need is still present. It is I now who gives the terrible cry, where are they?

Not everyone can leave hearth and home and go preach in a distant land. There will be family concerns such as health limitations or care-giving for elderly parents, etc. But if maintaining a comfortable home and two cars or staying close to mom or children or grandchildren are some of our priorities that come before our service to God and the needs of others, then we have failed in our faithfulness to God and to our husbands.

The needs of a preacher's wife

When a congregation asks our husband to serve as a preacher of God's Word, whether we are prepared for it or not, we become a part of his serving. As his wife, it is a place of privilege, but it is also a place that holds a lot of ambiguities. The difficulty is to try and maintain a balanced emotional equilibrium.

A preacher's wife has three needs and when these are met her balancing act becomes much easier:

- ◆ A need to belong, which should include trusted friendships, although these may not be found within the local congregation.
- ◆ A sense of self worth, to be valued for herself, recognized by her husband who is willing to share himself with her away from the concerns of his work.
- ◆ Clear and healthy expectations whereby her husband can let it be understood that he alone was asked to serve and anything that his wife adds to that is up to her.

I would be remiss if I did not also address the needs of the children of a preacher's family. The wife of a preacher has additional concerns in her faithful service toward her family because the children of a preacher can get lost in the shuffle of serving the constant needs in a congregation. Children thrive on a stable value system of righteousness and justice. A faithful mother will recognize that it will be her responsibility to make sure their family values are taught and maintained, Proverbs 6:20; 2 Timothy 1:5. This teaching and training must continue even during times of public worship. This will not only be good for her children, but they will not detract from the influence a good man must maintain within the congregation he serves.

Resolutions to be a faithful preacher's wife

Although a number of these points are not original with me and have been collected from different sources, we as preachers' wives would do well to adopt these resolutions. Consider choosing a resolution you are having difficulty with, concentrate on the Scripture and pray about the problem. Share your concern with your husband, seeking his advice and help.

- I will learn to adjust and find joy in new towns and new families of God, making the best of whatever situation we are in. Contentment will become a wonderful strength in my character, 1 Timothy 6:8; Philippians 4:11.

- Whenever possible, I will accompany my husband when he preaches/teaches away from home. I will rejoice in the privilege and understand the responsibility of being a supportive wife, 1 Corinthians 9:4; 1 Corinthians 7:2–5.

- If I am unable to accompany my husband, I will busy myself with the things only a good wife can accomplish for him: taking care of his children and creating a home that will welcome her husband's return. I will continue to be active and supportive in the local congregation, 1 Timothy 5:14.

♦   I will learn to hear my husband criticized without becoming angry even when unfavorable or unfair judgments are made. I will not hold on to past hurts which will develop into bitterness. I will balance my attitude with love and patience, 2 Timothy 2:24ff.

♦   I will try to adjust my wants to the monetary support my husband receives. I will seek ways to make the budget stretch so that our family is fed and clothed, Proverbs 31:10ff; Luke 3:14.

♦   I will work to grow in the grace and knowledge of our Lord and Savior, Jesus Christ, 2 Peter 3:18. Through my spiritual growth I will enjoy sharing mutual goals with my husband, 1 Peter 3:7.

♦   I will refer questions and guidance back to my husband when matters are raised that concern his role of preacher. I will maintain his leadership as my head, Ephesians 5:23–24.

♦   I will be a woman who loves others, a sacrifice of my heart, Matthew 22:39 — I will also understand the wisdom of many friendships, Romans 12:10.

♦   I will understand my tongue must be silent where my husband's work is concerned. I cannot gossip or share confidential information, 2 Thessalonians 3:11; Ephesians 4:29; Ecclesiastes 5:2.

♦   I will protect my husband's reputation. I may have to change my day's plan in order to accompany him to the home of a lone woman who seeks my husband's guidance, whether in a class or a counseling session, 1 Corinthians 9:5; 2 Peter 2:14.

♦ I will not become the *new broom*, sweeping old traditions out the door when my husband begins a new work. I will adjust and accommodate the needs of those my husband serves. I will be a supportive worker, rejoicing in the abilities of others, Romans 12:10; Philippians 2:3.

♦ I will recognize the good received from welcoming visitors and strangers into our home, Romans 12:13. I will recognize the wisdom of organization in my home, so that neither my husband nor I will be embarrassed when company suddenly comes to our door, Proverbs 31:10ff.

♦ I will not worry about what the previous preacher's wife did or didn't do. I will give thanks to God for my own individuality and capabilities, Romans 12:6–8.

♦ I will not frown or make gestures to correct any mistakes my husband makes while preaching or teaching. I will praise his efforts and rejoice with him. Privately, I will be honest with criticism, seasoned with salt, ensuring support and encouragement, 1 Corinthians 13:4–6.

♦ I will understand that as I grow older my confidence increases and this can sometimes intimidate younger women. I will continue to concentrate on humility, having a meek and quiet spirit, 1 Peter 3:4; 5:6.

♦ I will be thankful for the many, many gifts others offer me and my family. I will understand their gifts are not my reward for I have not earned them, Colossians 3:15.

♦ I will understand and accept that no matter what loving efforts I make as a preacher's wife, I will disappoint the expectations of some. I will concentrate on pleasing my husband and my Father in heaven, Galatians 1:10.

♦ I will encourage good attitudes by all concerned when my husband must step down in his service to a congregation. I will not participate in dividing the Lord's work, 1 Corinthians 1:11.

Truly, the faithful wife of a preacher of righteousness is a challenging role and we must be ever vigilant in our faithfulness toward God, our husbands, and all those we come in contact with. Let us pray for our husbands, for God knows the past and the future. Let us maintain a mutual goal of heaven, giving and receiving courage from each other in our walk with God.

F. D. Srygley wrote of T. B. Larimore and his wife, and specifically of all preachers' wives:

> He has accomplished great good, and his praise is in all the churches for his work's sake; but who has thought to consider the magnitude of her part in his labors, or sound abroad her praise for her labors of love and prayers of faith in furthering his good works? I would not take from his crown a single star to ornament hers; but I beseech you brethren, in common justice, to remember always to make the one crown of his praise encircle both their brows; for are not the twain one flesh? And what I say of these two made one, applies to every husband and wife in every station in life.

What Have **You** Done All Day?
—Homemaking—
by Becky Allen

The Big Question

Fix the breakfast, make the beds
Wash dirty faces, comb snarly heads
Scrub the floor and wax it too
Then put three loads of laundry through
Clean the stove that's caked with gook
Then put the supper on to cook
Set the table, comb my hair
Put on my face, no time to spare
The house is shining, the kids are clean
Supper's ready, everything gleams
He comes through the door and what does he say?
"Hi, Sweetie, what did you do all day?"
—{ **by Donna Carroll Batton** }—

Higher Expectations

When you think of homemaking what picture comes to mind? A perfect home with everything spic and span, neat and organized, prim and proper children quietly reading a book, ever ready meal placed on the table for husband or company? HA! Not in our home! Maybe there are some wonderful ladies out there that can accomplish this on an everyday basis, but I know there are those of us that struggle just to keep the place picked up, children from yelling at each other and getting everyone in one place long enough to have a meal together.

We have all heard the expression *home is where the heart is*. Making your house a home is more than the physical appearance. It is more about the heart. I believe this can mean different things to different families. We all have different schedules, needs, etc. and we must learn what works best for our family. There is no one mold we should have to try to fit in just for the sake of living up to a certain persona. I have learned that if I try to always be just like someone else then I am going to fail.

I know that as preachers' wives, we are sometimes placed in a different category. Many try to put us on a level where expectations are very high in our overall organization of the home and how our children behave. Unfortunately, this is something that will probably never go away. People watching us through a magnifying glass and living in a fishbowl will always be something we have to deal with. Sometimes I want to tell them, just because I married a preacher doesn't mean I am somehow magically turned into June Cleaver. Even though it can be very frustrating at times, high standards can also help me to stay on track, if I let them. We do need a sense of accountability in keeping a decent house, our children under control, and in providing a place that our husbands want to come home to.

So, What Can We Do?

Even matters as *simple* as keeping a home can cause strife if we do not set standards. We must look to Scripture for guidance in our role as a wife and mother. God expects a godly home and we need to do everything in our power to provide that for our family. We must make our family realize that the divine expectation in Scripture can only be met when each member of the family works together. We need to remember the following verses and put them into practice. "*Wives, submit to your own husbands, as is fitting in the Lord. Husbands, love your wives and do not be bitter toward them. Children, obey your parents in all things, for this is well pleasing to the Lord,*" Colossians 3:18–20. If we will learn to have a servant's heart like our Lord, then we will all be able to take these verses to heart and practice them. A great motto for any home can be found in the latter reading of Joshua 24:15, "*But as for me and my house, we will serve the Lord.*" Nothing greater can a house stand upon than on the Lord.

Ladies First . . .

If you are like me, you might ask yourself questions like these: "Why is it so hard for him to put his shoes away? Why can't he put his dishes in the dishwasher? Why can't he see the crumbs all over the floor?" and the questions could go on and on. The Holy Spirit says, "*Wives, submit to your own husbands, as is fitting in the Lord*" and "*let the wife see that she respects her husband,*" Colossians 3:18; Ephesians 5:33b. Why is it that this is so hard to do sometimes? Of course it can make a big difference, depending on what your husband is like. If your husband is passive, easy going, helpful, etc., being submissive may be easier for you than someone who is married to a man that is more particular, outspoken, and not as willing to help at home. The latter does not give us the excuse to be rebellious in our duties or toward our husbands.

We need to have pride in our homes and remember they are a blessing from God. What does an unkempt home say about our thankfulness for what we have been blessed with? We need to remember that our thankfulness is not dependent on others but rather a reflection of ourselves. If we are constantly griping about what everyone else is *not* doing, then we are taking time away from what *we* should be doing. We must not look for excuses or blame everyone else. I am not saying that wives should never ask their husbands for help or expect their children to do chores. It would be more profitable to take a step back and review our intentions. Sometimes we may have a valid reason for griping, but most of the time it is probably just out of habit. This is where we women get the rap for being nags. I have done it and I am sure many of you have as well.

If we are not careful, we can unknowingly cause members of our family to resent us. Instead, we need to make sure we are communicating with our family what we need, what is expected, and how to make it all work. This communication should be different for each family member. When we talk to our husbands like they are our children, they will not respond kindly, Ephesians 5:33b. When speaking to our younger children as if they were older, they will not understand; and if we speak to our older children as a 2 year old, it will only demean their intelligence.

Perhaps the best tool of communication is to have an old fashioned *sit down* with your family. This is a great time to lay out all household needs. Taking time to look at everyone's activities will help greatly in preparing a schedule for different chores. It is profitable to have this schedule written down in plain sight for all to see. That way, no one can say they forgot or didn't know what they were supposed to be doing. For children, it might also be helpful to have a reward system. I like to think of it this way: if you catch your children doing chores on their own without being told, give them recognition or even a reward. This could be anything from a hug and a thank you to taking them for an ice cream or to a movie. When you have to tell your child to do a chore, treat it like a real job in the real world. This will help build their sense of responsibility. Do the work, get paid. No work, no pay. This does not have to be a large amount of money and should reflect the age of the child, the nature of the work, and how well the job was done. Children feel a sense of pride when they receive their reward. Now, having said all this, I am not one who feels that kids should be paid for every little thing you ask them to do. They need to understand that being part of a family means you work together as a family and there are just certain things that are expected of them.

Wives and mothers have been given great responsibilities that God knew only women could handle. We need to be thankful for the position God put us in and know that being submissive to our husbands is not demeaning but rather empowering. God knew what He was doing and knows where our talents naturally lie. Women have great minds and capabilities just as men do! When we use them according to the will of the Father we will be successful in our endeavors whether at home, work, or play!

OK, Men . . .

I know this is a book for preacher's wives, but I think it would be helpful if husbands read this as well. Since husbands are to dwell with their wives in understanding (1 Peter 3:7a), they have great responsibilities. God calls for them to be head of the house, providers of physical needs, and the spiritual leaders of the family. They set the precedent for everything inside the home. Husbands have been commanded to *"... love (their) wives and do not be bitter toward them,"* Colossians 3:19. They need to have patience and understanding with their spouse. Peter reminds us that wives are *"the weaker vessel, and as being heirs together of the grace of life...,"* 1 Peter 3:7b. God calls women the weaker vessel yet the husband and wife are heirs together! Just because women are of a gentler spirit does not mean they should be treated like children or as if they are stupid. Women possess intelligent minds and are fully capable of making certain decisions. However, women are not infallible and do require help from their husbands. Just as men come home from work ready to do nothing, some wives feel the same way. Whether they work outside the home or not, they still have been working. They have been busy getting the kids ready for the day, doing laundry, doing the dishes, cleaning toilets, making beds, vacuuming, sweeping, buying groceries, the list goes on and on! Women who work outside the home and have all of these things yet to do when they get off work need their husband's help even more!

I really like this poem by Laura Leigh Fields and would like to share it with you:

I Have Had It!

I have had it with the cleaning.
It is all I ever get done.
I'm taking a vacation.
I need to have fun.
I am not going to lift another finger.

I don't care if the place falls apart at the seams.
I am not a maid.
I will no longer clean.
The sinks are full of dishes.
There is something spilt in the floor.
I pretend not to notice.
I'm not cleaning anymore.
The trash needs to be taken out.
The windows should be cleaned.
I don't care if it all piles up.
I'm not doing another thing!
The bathtub has a ring around it.
All the clothes I own are in a pile.
Weeks go by; I'm still on strike.
I look around with a worried smile.
I think they will buckle before I do.
I know my family won't live in filth.
But the weeks turn into months,
If I don't do it, no one will.
The yard is starting to grow around me.
All I can see is weeds.
The pool is turning a glossy green,
The bottom you can no longer see.
I am so tired of being under appreciated,
But the filth is killing me too.
I think I better get started.
It looks like I have a lot to do.

Most likely many wives have felt just the same as this poem describes. Cooperation is necessary from everyone in the household to make things work. If all family members are willing, you can have your home running like a well-oiled machine. Husbands can do a lot in helping their wives be all they can be!

Now for the Kids . . .

If kids today only knew how good they have it! I once told my kids about the way disobedient children were treated in the Old Testament, Deuteronomy 21:18–21. Yeah, it didn't work. We need to have control over our children. They need to understand their position in the family and that they are expected to abide by our rules. Children need to be taught that God is to be put first in their lives and in their family. They must be *shown* God's word on the subject of parents and children. *"Children, obey your parents in the Lord, for this is right. Honor your father and mother, which is the first commandment with promise,"* Ephesians 6:1–2. This eternal truth is driven home through our example. If parents do not show respect and love for one another, then children will not show respect and love. If they do not see mom and dad helping each other and working together both inside and outside the home, then they will not have a basis for these qualities.

"This hurts me more than it hurts you." Does that stir up certain memories for you like it does me? Disciplining our children is not pleasant but necessary. *"Train up a child in the way he should go, and when he is old he will not depart from it,"* Proverbs 22:6. *"He who spares his rod hates his son, But he who loves him disciplines him promptly,"* Proverbs 13:24. Trying to explain this to your kids while you are spanking them can seem futile. I love my children dearly and do not like having to punish them. But I realize they do have to learn and I must be willing to teach them even if it means spanking, taking their favorite things away, or grounding them.

> *Just because I married a preacher doesn't mean I am somehow magically turned into June Cleaver.*

We must be careful not to succumb to the ways of the world that allows kids to run the house. Remember, God put you in charge! If we do not expect our children to behave properly, then we are not being the kind of parents God wants us to be. We are told in Psalm 127:3, *"Behold, children are a heritage from the Lord, The fruit of the womb is a reward."* If we do not believe that our children are a reward, then we will not raise them in the *"training and admonition of the Lord,"* Ephesians 6:4b. Children play just as important a role in the family as everyone else. They can be a vital part to the heart and inner workings of the household. We must nurture them and prepare them for the world in which we live. This requires them to learn responsibility and good work ethics. We can establish these qualities in the home and as a mom it is your challenge to do so.

Let's discuss the touchy subject of *preachers' kids*. Many have been given a bad rap! They are often given a higher standard to live by and impossible expectations are placed upon them. Many forget they are kids and will make mistakes. They are scrutinized under a higher-powered microscope than other children within the congregation. This can be very frustrating for both parents and children. Children can become so discouraged that they dread going to Bible class and worship services. We, as their parents, must encourage their desire to focus on God and not on the negativity thrown their way. Don't get me wrong, our kids need to be doing God's will and acting appropriately. We need to teach them to… "Do your best and let God take care of the rest!"

A Good Idea

One thing I came across while researching for this chapter was the idea of a homemaking journal by Dionna Sanchez. Homemaking Journals were actually passed down through generations in the *olden days*. It is a journal where you record in one place all things related to homemaking. In the journal you can put:

- ◆ Recipes (especially beloved family recipes)
- ◆ Inspirational poems, quotes, Bible verses or excerpts that inspire

your love for family, home, and homemaking.

♦ Tips, tricks, hints, and ideas to help your home run smoothly.
♦ Home Schooling information
♦ Health and First Aid remedies & tricks
♦ Ideas and tips for emergency preparedness
♦ List of birthdates and anniversaries
♦ Holiday traditions
♦ Kid stuff (activities, projects, and kid recipes)
♦ Gardening — planting info, seasonal planting favorites, tips, tricks
♦ Seasonal tips — helpful info on what to do before and after each season
♦ Your daily routines
♦ Meal planning
♦ Budget outline
♦ Trusted numbers of doctors, dentists, builders, etc.

When you put together your Homemaker's Journal, turn it into a labor of love. Make it something to be treasured and cherished to hand down. This can become a valuable resource. Whether you give it to your daughters when they move into their first home, your daughter-in-law when she marries your son, or a special niece, this idea is a real winner in creating a homemaking legacy.

Homemaking is one of the greatest things we can do in this life. It gives us the opportunity to be a loving wife, a caring mother, a teacher and nurse to both the physical and spiritual body. As the wife of a gospel preacher let us never forget the great responsibility to women. We can let God use us as an example in our respective congregations and communities by the way we live, handle our children and our homes. Don't let anyone tell you that your job as a mom or housewife is not important or not a real job because it is! Being able to juggle so many different activities is heroic!

Being a preacher's wife has meant many different things throughout my married years as I am sure it has for you. It has brought great joy and meaningful relationships but has also torn me down and cut me to the heart. But I find comfort in knowing that my Lord and Savior believes in me and my abilities so much that he blessed me with a good husband and two beautiful children! Thank you God for making me a homemaker!

•   "The Big Question" by Donna Batton. Used by permission of the author.
•   "I've Had It!" by Laura Leigh Fields. Used by permission of the author.

Come on to My House
—Hospitality—
by Cindy DeBerry

T hirty-five years ago I was a young wife with three beautiful little girls. Life was very good. Royce was working at Caterpillar Tractor Company making good money. He was preaching one Sunday a month for a small congregation and filling in other places as needed. We had a Bible study in our home with other members of our congregation once a week. I was busy with my sweet babies. I was very comfortable. I was happy, and then the bomb dropped. Royce said, "Honey, I want to go into preaching full-time." WHAT??????????? I can't be a preacher's wife! I am not qualified! I don't have any wisdom! I don't know enough! I am an introvert. I can't talk to everybody! HELP!! Royce was very encouraging, saying all the things I wanted to hear but still didn't believe. How could I successfully meet this challenge? The answer for meeting any challenge successfully is one action at a time. If hospitality seems as overwhelming to you as it did to me, may I suggest it is done the same way, one action at a time.

First: Figure out what we are talking about

When someone speaks of hospitality, we tend to think of dinner parties, game nights, and general socializing. We are inviting someone out of their comfortable home with a full pantry to come to our comfortable home to recreate and enjoy our pantry for a change. While that can certainly be one aspect of hospitality, it merely scratches the surface of the biblical definition. We need to consider the Greek words and their meanings.

One of the Greek words translated hospitality in the Bible is *philoxeos*. This word is really two words combined. The first part is from *philos*, a primitive word meaning "beloved, dear, or friendly." The second part is from *xenos*, a primitive word meaning "foreign, a foreigner, guest." Thus, *philoxeos* is defined as "loving strangers." In 1 Timothy 3:2, the word hospitality is translated from the Greek word *xenodocheo*. Again, this word is really two words combined. The first part is from the primitive word *xenos* which means "foreign, a foreigner, guest." The second part is from *dechomai* which is a primitive verb meaning "to receive." Thus *xenodocheo* is defined "to entertain strangers." So the biblical definition is talking about "loving or entertaining strangers."

Second: Look for New Testament passages using the word

What are the passages that speak of hospitality commanding us today? 1Timothy 3:2 and Titus 1:8 list hospitality as a qualification for a man to become an overseer in the Lord's church. 1 Timothy 5:9–10 shows that a widow could not be considered a widow in deed unless she had *"shown hospitality to strangers"* and *"washed the saints' feet."* In Romans 12:1, Paul is urging the Christians in Rome *"to present your bodies a living and holy sacrifice, acceptable to God."* Verses 10–18 give us a great overview of a hospitable attitude:

> *Be devoted to one another in brotherly love; give prefer-*
> *ence to one another in honor; not lagging behind in dili-*
> *gence, fervent in spirit, serving the Lord; rejoicing in hope,*
> *persevering in tribulation, devoted to prayer, contribut-*
> *ing to the needs of the saints, practicing hospitality. Bless*
> *those who persecute you; bless and curse not. Rejoice with*
> *those who rejoice, and weep with those who weep. Be of*
> *the same mind toward one another; do not be haughty in*
> *mind, but associate with the lowly. Do not be wise in your*
> *own estimation. Never pay back evil for evil to anyone.*
> *Respect what is right in the sight of all men. If possible, so*
> *far as it depends on you, be at peace with all men.*

Hebrews 13:2 commands us not to neglect *"to show hospitality to strangers, for by this some have entertained angels without knowing it."* Matthew 25:31–46 reveals that we could lose our home in heaven because we have not shown hospitality. 1 Peter 4:9 adds that we should *"be hospitable to one another without complaint."*

Third: Look for Biblical examples

Now that we have examined the Greek words for hospitality and looked at the New Testament passages using the words, let's consider some scriptural examples within God's word of loving or entertaining strangers.

In Genesis 18, three men arrived at the home of Abraham and Sarah. We are told that Abraham *"ran from the tent door to meet them, and bowed himself to the earth."* He did not know these men and he did not know what their business was but he welcomed them to his home. In verse three, Abraham says, *"My lord, if now I have found favor in your sight, please do not pass your servant by."* Verse four goes on, *"Please let a little water be brought and wash your feet, and rest yourselves under the tree; and I will bring a piece of bread, that you may refresh yourselves: after that you may go on, since you have visited your servant."* When the guests agreed to stay, the next few verses show Abraham *hurried* to the tent and told Sarah to *quickly* prepare a feast for the visitors. Then Abraham *"ran to the herd, and took a tender and choice calf and gave it to the servant; and he hurried to prepare it."* We have a picture of two people going all out to make sure their guests had every comfort they had available. Abraham and Sarah were showing hospitality. They lived in a tent but they offered what they had, an attitude of respect, shade to rest in, water to wash their feet, and food to eat as quickly as they could prepare it.

In 2 Kings 4:8–10, *"…Elisha passed over to Shunem, where there was a prominent woman, and she persuaded him to eat food. And so it was, as often as he passed by, he turned in there to eat food. And she said to her husband, 'Behold now, I perceive that this is a holy man of God passing by us continually. Please, let us make a little walled upper chamber and let us set a bed for him there, and a table and a chair and a lampstand, and it shall be, when he comes to us, that he can turn in there.'"* The necessity of food, shelter, and rest has not changed through the ages. This woman was thinking with a hospitable heart, anticipating the needs of her guest before he arrived.

In Acts 16:14–15, Lydia is converted and says to Paul, *"'If you have judged me to be faithful to the Lord, come into my house and stay.' And she prevailed upon us."* Later when Paul wrote the letter to the Philippians he says, *"I thank my God in all my remembrance of you, always offering prayer with joy in my every prayer for you all, in view of your participation in the gospel from the first day until now,"* Philippians 1:3–5. Lydia was the one who begged them to come to her house and stay that first day and according to Philippians she was still seeing to Paul's needs. If our acts of hospitality can be considered participating in the gospel, what is our lack of hospitality considered?

We can see that God through the ages has given us examples of people involved in hospitality. We can see that in every age food and shelter were key components in giving hospitality. We could look at hospitality as providing others with things they need but do not presently have available. The key to having a hospitable heart is our attitude. Our attitude should reflect respect and compassion for our guest, whatever their situation. In view of all the passages we noticed above, we can see why God's people were always begging for opportunities to give hospitality. We, likewise, should be standing in line praying for opportunities to show our hospitality.

Fourth: Personal application

We see from these examples it doesn't take a lot to show hospitality. Water, food, the shade of a tree, a table and chair, a bed, a lamp stand, etc. are all things available to most of us blessed to live in America.

However, as we will see, there are times even in America that people have simple needs that they cannot meet themselves. When brethren stand up and offer these things, it is a life altering experience for both parties. Actually, the key to loving or entertaining strangers is simply to put other's needs above our own. Hospitality is usually thought of as something we do where we live. 1 Samuel 25:2–39 shows that Abigail showed hospitality *on the road, bringing* food to David and his men. We need to ask ourselves the question, are we squandering precious opportunities?

My daddy died of pancreatic cancer in 1971. His ordeal lasted fifteen months. We wanted him home. Unfortunately, my mom, eight year old brother and I, at age thirteen, could not physically meet all of his needs. The Westside congregation in Aurora, Illinois, arranged a signup sheet. One member of the congregation came to our home at ten p.m. and stayed until two a.m. At two a.m. they were relieved by another who signed up for the 2:00 AM – 6:00 AM shift. My mother could sleep from ten p.m. until six a.m. every night. Another couple signed to come for four hours one evening a week and on Saturdays. This was our grocery shopping, *whatever needed to be done* time. During our fifteen month ordeal there was **never** a shift that was not covered. We did not ask for this; it was offered by our brethren.

This extreme hospitality shown to my family had a huge impact. I never had a chance to repay these people; we moved away when Royce started preaching. What I figured out early on is hospitality is a circle. You do what you can for those who need it and the circle continues.

Let's start simply. What about the visiting preacher invited to our congregation to preach for a few days? Most congregations put up an empty meal list and let the members fill in the meal they would like to provide. One empty space on this list is a disgrace to the **entire** congregation. Every example of hospitality given in God's word uses language such as *"prevailed upon"* or *"begged us to stay."* Have you ever seen a line formed at the sign-up sheet to feed the preacher? Lydia worked and did not have a dishwasher, refrigerator, or microwave available. Sarah had to wait while Abraham had dinner killed; then she cooked it. We can go to our freezer, defrost and cook. We can also take advantage of the many choices in the grocery stores for pre-prepared foods. Salads may be purchased ready to put in a bowl. Meats may be purchased ready to serve; add baked potatoes and a veggie and you have a meal. There are cookbooks available with many quick semi-homemade dishes. Remember Abigail? Have dinner on the road at a restaurant. When feeding our guests, remember to feed their hearts along with their stomachs. The time to become better acquainted through conversation is as important to an individual as the physical sustenance. I fear some of our good reasons for not opening our homes will not sound so good on the Day of Judgment. A few personal touches could make a big difference. Ask if there are dietary restrictions and write them at the top of the list so everyone may prepare accordingly. Through the years I have eaten in many homes and I can tell you I don't remember what people served but I do remember the attitude bestowed.

> *I fear some of our good reasons for not opening our homes will not sound so good on the Day of Judgment.*

Beyond providing the meals, someone needs to open their home and invite this man in for the week. As the wives of preachers, most of us have been on the giving and receiving end of this situation. What do we need available to be ready for this challenge? Let me suggest that all we need today are the same things made available to Elisha. A room with a bed, table, chair, and lamp is all anyone needs to be quite comfortable. If we think with a hospitable heart, we can pick up notebooks, pens, stamps, trial size items, etc. to place on the table for our guest's use. The simple gesture of a vase with flowers from your garden adds a welcoming presence. This all relays the message of comfort. It says welcome home while you are here. Cleanliness is also important. We had the opportunity to stay in a beautiful spacious suite within someone's home. Decorating the room had obviously taken up much time and money. The furniture was expensive and new. One glance around the room and we knew we were going to be very comfortable. Everything was beautiful to the eye. That night we pulled the covers down and as we started to crawl into this inviting bed, we saw that the sheets were very obviously soiled. At that moment nothing else mattered in the room. We didn't want to sleep in that bed, didn't want to embarrass our host, and didn't know what to do. Clean sheets are something I had always taken for granted! I now realize clean sheets are the most important factor to the guest's comfort zone!

Sometimes college kids come through our hometown needing a safe place to rest. What a golden opportunity to get to know a Christian from another locale. We can have an influence on these young people that may reach into the next generation of the Lord's church. No need to worry about having anything in common with them. Young people generally love to talk, so by simply listening we are telling them how important they are to us and the Lord's work. Hospitality is more than sharing a meal. When conversation is lagging, ask your guest a question about their hometown. Questions about things they know or are familiar with shows you care about them and their experiences. Add a pizza delivery and everyone is happy!

One day, we received a phone call from a man we had never met. We talked for a few minutes and realized he was the son-in-law of a couple we knew from a congregation where Royce's dad had worked. He had been transferred to our city and needed a place to stay while working to get his family a home so they could all move here. We invited him into our home to stay for the few weeks it took to accomplish his goals. We all benefited from the relationship that grew from this chance job transfer.

We have received phone calls from family members whose loved ones were being transferred from their small city hospital to our capital city hospital. This family was facing a life and death situation with their loved one and needed a haven to take care of their own need for food, shelter, and clean clothing. Don't forget to offer your washer and dryer. The only thing worse than sitting in a waiting room all day worrying about a loved one is doing so in dirty clothes!

We worked with a congregation that had two families who lived on the Kankakee River. You have not experienced a slumber party until you have stayed up all night watching the levee, praying the sandbags hold back the rising waters. We had been at it for seven days. When the levee broke and the flood waters came, this family watched everything they had be washed away. This family of four joined the six of us in our double wide trailer for a few weeks (yes, just one bathroom!) while we waited for the flood waters to recede and then cleaned up the mess afterward. They had a dog and we had a child with allergies, so we were using our backyard shed for the dog. A tornado came through and put his home in a tree (we can't explain how, but the dog was not hurt); so a member of the congregation made a doghouse. This protected him from the *blizzard* (spring is unpredictable in the Midwest) the next week. We were all looking for the positive things in each of these situations, so Larry made snow cream and we all enjoyed big bowls! Sharing and caring are a blessing to all people.

Fires and tornados are destructive. Brethren who come to the aid of others find greater blessings as givers than do the receivers. One family lost everything one New Years Day to a fire. They had family members to stay with but no insurance. Brethren from all over the state worked together to gather what they needed. At another congregation a family lost their home and most of their belongings to a tornado. This family with two small children had nothing but the clothes on their back and whatever happened to be in their car. They too, had family members to stay with and insurance to fix the house but needed clothes and personal items immediately to get by until the insurance could send an adjuster out and settle the claim. Every situation is different with unique needs. Acts 4:32 has a deeper meaning after helping someone through such situations.

Another family sold their home faster than they could get possession of their new home. They moved in with us for two months while they waited for their new home to be available. They were older and we had young children. Our children enjoyed having *grandparents* around all the time (ours lived out of state, as do most preachers). If we are looking for the good, we can find it in any situation. I learned different recipes that we still enjoy today!

When parents have medical situations or funerals to deal with we could show them hospitality by opening our homes to their nervous and confused little people. My uncle passed away when I was ten and my parents went to Tennessee for the funeral. I stayed with the preacher's family and remember being afraid and very nervous. It was Mother's Day weekend and I was away from my mother for the first time in my life. Sister Gwen Belue was so soft spoken and kind! I don't remember what we ate, or what the furniture looked like, but forty-five years later I can recall her attitude towards me and how safe it made me feel. Gather a small suitcase or box and put crayons, stickers you get in your junk mail, color books (go to the dollar store), a pad of paper, envelopes, a roll of tape, etc., and you can keep a child's mind busy for an entire afternoon. Add some old magazines (to cut out pictures), scissors, and a glue stick and encourage them to make get well or sympathy cards for their loved ones. Everybody needs a purpose. Provide the supplies and they will work constructively.

It is imperative the rules are explained to any guest, but especially the young people. The first place Royce tried out to preach full time taught me this lesson. We arrived in the home and the family was very friendly, until one of our daughters climbed up to sit on the couch. I had instructed her to go in and sit down, so she was following directions. She had sat on the *adult* couch instead of the *children's* couch. We had never

been in a home with designated couches before. Inform your guests before a touchy situation causes embarrassment around the room. Most
guests do not wish to offend the customs nor the sensitivities of their
hosts. They just need to be informed. Announce specifics at the beginning. For instance, when the little ones arrive, the hostess could point out
their *special* couch and the children would know what was expected of
them. After the prayer has been said, the host might say, "Help yourself
to the dish in front of you and pass to the left." Everyone is then on the
same page and feels confident about what to do. Different cultures have
different customs and sensitivities. (You guessed right, Royce didn't get a
job offer that weekend!)

While it is important to remember the little ones, we can't forget
the adults in similar situations. Waiting all night (sometimes all week)
in the intensive care waiting room can be excruciating. We were camped
out for a week there before Royce's father passed away. The hospitality
shown will never be forgotten. Food and snacks brought to the waiting
room helped us sustain ourselves when no one wanted to leave. The roll
of quarters donated helped with the *need to have chocolate* moments.
The puzzle left for us gave us something to do in the long hours waiting.
Simple things that we could not provide for ourselves were brought by
brethren who cared enough. Priceless!

Our most unique (and my favorite) opportunity for hospitality
came when a member of our congregation had a situation in which her
three children were removed and put into foster care. This was our time
to step up to the plate to offer our hospitality. Three families from our
congregation, licensed with the state, opened our homes to these children. We were providing what they were lacking. We had three daughters and one son. Our son thought everything that was wrong in his life
was because he didn't have a brother. We licensed to keep the little boy
that was the same age as our son. He was so excited to finally have a
brother. This lasted about two months and then he decided everything
that was wrong in his life was because he had a brother. What a valuable

lesson Mike learned. Without this opportunity he would have missed this life lesson to realize the grass is not greener on the other side. Six months later the three children and their mother were reunited. This dear sister is still worshipping with this congregation to the glory of God some twenty plus years later. We were then asked to foster another child and have had the opportunity to foster around forty more through the years. The foster care curriculum has a chapter that would be great for everyone to consider when getting ready to give hospitality. One exercise has you write down your ten favorite things. First they tell you to choose eight to keep, then six, etc. until you are left with one or none of your ten favorite things. Now really—just think about how you would feel to lose most of what is important to you. This is how a stranger feels in someone else's home. They don't know what to expect for meals, free time, etc. It makes them feel like they are at your mercy. Show them around the house, point out where the essentials are, give them permission to take care of their own needs (here are the snack foods, sandwich fixings, etc., feel free to come and get whatever you want whenever you need to) and make them feel at home.

Quite often overlooked is our older generation. As we age we cannot always meet our own needs. When we put our older loved ones in a long term care facility instead of inviting them into our home, we have forfeited an opportunity to bestow hospitality. My mother lived with us for fourteen years after she was widowed. She had a little apartment within our home. She then met and married a wonderful Christian from a town about an hour and a half away. When she announced her plans one of our little ones asked, "Can she do that?" (She had lived with us when our four youngest girls were born so they didn't know life any other way, but when they figured out they got a grandpa out of the deal they were very excited!) When she moved out, a retired minister and his wife moved in and the circle continues. Royce's mom has an apartment on the other side of our house. Royce's aunt lived with us after her stroke for two years until she passed away. All of these older loved ones have needed our help; however, they have given us so much in return! They have more time for reading books and baking cookies for the littlest generation. I think they enjoy having each other to talk and work with. There are times that a facility is necessary for one reason or another; however, facilities are grossly overused in our society. When they are necessary, don't forget the opportunities for hospitality that will come from that scenario. We need to evaluate our attitudes and remember 1 Timothy 5:4.

Needs that are sprung upon us quickly without the opportunity to plan and prepare can be harrowing experiences. What about small spaces? If seating is a problem, kids love a picnic; put an old blanket on the floor and you have a picnic (the kids will smile and remember this meal, guaranteed). What about no guest room? Let two children share a room making it a special honor bestowed upon the child getting to prepare their room for the guest. Make it a fun challenge instead of drudgery. How can I stretch dinner to feed extra people? To remain calm and to be able to make your guests feel welcome, we need to have that hospitable heart ahead of time. Plan and you will be prepared. Prepare extra and freeze what is not eaten for dinner tonight. Now you are ready. (See, that wasn't hard!) When the opportunity presents itself, just thaw and add to the dinner table. Put an extra potato in the pot (my kids said I had to put that one in because they have heard me say it so many times). Add a third veggie or a salad to the meal and you are ready to feed extra people. Peanut butter and jelly can taste delicious when served with love and compassion. Small crowded homes with a happy caring atmosphere feel cozy.

It seems like our needs for hospitality are often times of trial, but there are also happy times that could use some hospitality. A new baby born into a family is a time of rejoicing! We can rejoice with those who are rejoicing by bringing dinner to the family while mom is recuperating. I know of a sister who had all of her sons and families surprise her for her 60th birthday. Her precious sisters in Christ delivered food to her family for three days. By meeting this need, everyone could enjoy their time together without worrying about what they were going to eat. They were rejoicing with her. Her reaction was, "What a treasure!"

When people have a need for hospitality, usually the preacher's phone number is the first found when they look up the local congregation. Since we are usually the first line of communication, we determine if this family feels wanted or unwanted. We certainly can share the love by involving other families in our congregation, talking beforehand to those who are open to hospitality so when the opportunity avails itself, we know who to call. Different seasons of life work better with different types of hospitality. Older couples usually have more time, space, and resources. When children are involved, a younger family would probably already have the equipment necessary. Working together will ensure meeting everyone's needs. There are so many ways to show hospitality. Hopefully, if hospitality has made you nervous in the past, this will be your first step in looking for your unique opportunities! Paul says in 1 Corinthians 9:22 that he had *"become all things to all men, that I may by all means save some."* We are blessed to be married to men with this same attitude. Our hospitable hearts will hold up their hands as they work to build up the Lord's church and the circle continues!

[All scriptures are from the New American Standard Bible. *Greek words and definitions are from* New American Standard Exhaustive Concordance of the Bible, *Holman Publishers, Nashville, Tennessee. Copyright 1981 The Lockman Foundation.]*

Mirror, Mirror on the Wall . . .
—Your Appearance Reflects Your Heart—
by Julie Roberts

I grabbed the hanger in frustration and trudged toward the Wal-Mart cashier to purchase what I considered to be the ugliest pair of shorts I had ever owned. As I pulled out my checkbook, I thought to myself, "Oh, what does it matter?"

As a brand-new, nineteen-year-old Christian, I was facing my first modesty test. My boyfriend was working as a preaching intern for the summer, and he had invited me to join him and about fifty other Christians on a white-water rafting trip. Having never met any of the members of his congregation, I wanted to make a good impression. The problem was that I had no idea how to dress modestly for a rafting trip.

I knew that simply wearing my swimsuit was out of the question, but it was a very hot summer, and I didn't want to wear jeans down the river. Capri pants were out of style and not easy to find, and so I spent hours searching for shorts I deemed long enough to be appropriate. Now I had finally found a long pair, but to my nineteen-year-old fashion sensibilities, they were exceedingly ugly. And to add insult to injury, I was purchasing them at Wal-Mart—not exactly the fashion Mecca of the world.

A few days later, I was having breakfast with the rafting group, feeling a bit strange and unattractive dressed in my new *modest* attire. I was shocked when the first two girls who approached me to introduce themselves gave me a compliment.

"We just love your shorts!" they gushed. "They are so modest. Where did you find them?"

I decided right then that I must have passed the test. Not only that, but I learned a valuable lesson: Appearance matters. People notice.

As Christian Women, Our Appearance Matters

Our appearance matters, because it cannot be hidden. As Christians—and especially as preachers' wives—people take notice of how we conduct ourselves, and they have very high expectations. Most people may never find out if we've neglected taking food to a certain widow. Perhaps only a few will hear a bit of gossip that slipped from our tongues. But everyone we meet will notice our appearance.

Most of us put careful consideration into our appearance, as it is a reflection of our personality and sense of style. However, we sometimes forget that our appearance reflects on much more than that. Our appearance reflects on our husbands and families, as well. A successful man wants to proudly introduce his attractive and well-kept wife to others. A child is embarrassed if he is the only kid whose mom picks him up from school wearing baggy pajamas and house slippers.

Most importantly, as public figures and Christians, our appearance is a reflection of the gospel. When we mention that we are a Christian, introduce ourselves as the preacher's wife, or share our faith with a neighbor, our appearance is the packaging in which that message arrives.

Not only does our appearance send a visible message, but it can also lead others to sin. Obviously, immodest dress can entice men to think impure thoughts. It seems no Bible class on modesty is complete without a reference to Matthew 5:28, where we learn that when a man lusts after a woman, he has committed adultery in his heart. It even says he would be better off plucking out the eye that caused him to sin than to lose his soul because of it. But as women, we should not be so naïve as to think that our appearance can lead only men to sin. We should recognize how much we personally struggle with the first few verses of Matthew 7, *"Judge not, that you be not judged...."* When we notice a woman who is showing too much cleavage, is our first thought, "Oh that poor dear! Surely she is unaware that she is exposed! I must inform her of her predicament so that she can run and cover herself?" Most likely, not. Our initial reactions are probably not quite as forgiving and charitable. Neither are those of our sisters in Christ who will judge us on our appearance. We should not allow ourselves to be a stumbling block to them.

How Do We Recognize a Problem with Our Appearance?

It's easy to pat ourselves on the back for our modest attire when we compare our outfits with those of women we see in the world. For instance, it's noticeable when we are one of the few families at the restaurant on Sunday who have obviously dressed up and been to church that morning. When we judge ourselves by these standards, we may reason that our appearance and attire are just fine.

"You are the light of the world. A city that is set on a hill cannot be hidden," Matthew 5:14. We need to be *set apart* and *shine as a light* in the world, and our appearance should reflect this. Hopefully, the way we dress makes us stand out to the lost. Our attire should be a refreshing oasis of purity, modesty, class, and self-respect in a world of sensuality, pride, and decadence. We must be careful, however, that we are not solely judging our appearance by worldly standards, but by God's.

If our appearance truly reflects God's desires for us, then we will most likely stand out in the world. However, this also means that our appearance probably *shouldn't* make us stand out in a room full of Christians. If we're searching our hearts to determine whether we are struggling with a problem related to our appearance, we should start by comparing ourselves to other sisters-in-Christ. Take notice of the most righteous women you know, for whom you hold the most respect. The next time you are gathered together with a group of these women, see if you stand out. Are you showing the most skin? Are you wearing the most expensive designer clothes or jewelry? Are you the only woman at the worship service wearing jeans? If so, ask yourself why this is happening so that you can better understand and address the situation.

Our Appearance Reflects Our Hearts

It saddens us to see a child with a bandana covering a bald head, a sallow complexion, and a sheen to their skin. We are saddened, because we recognize the outward signs of chemotherapy, which we know is fighting a deadly disease within. Much like physical illness, our spiritual health reveals itself through symptoms and signs. External problems are only indicators of a hidden, internal weakness or illness.

"For as he thinks in his heart, so is he," Proverbs 23:7. When it comes to our appearance, we must understand that an outward problem has an inward cause. The question becomes, what is the problem? By dressing inappropriately, are we intentionally sinning? Or are we simply ignorant of God's word and don't realize the problems our appearance is creating? Either way, the message we are sending to those around us is that we are spiritually weak. We need to admit that our outward appearance is a mirror of what's going on in our hearts. We need to take a look in that mirror and *"examine ourselves,"* 2 Corinthians 13:5.

Take a Look in the Mirror: Am I Overdressed?

Have you ever seen an evangelist's wife who was dressed completely over the top—too much make-up, too much hair, too many jewels? If not, then you clearly don't have access to the Christian Broadcasting Network on your television. Sadly, many women in *Christian television* exemplify what *not* to do when it comes to our appearance. Surely when these women first learned they would be seen on television by millions of viewers, they simply wanted to dress up and look their best. However, by overdoing it, they have become yet another caricature and stereotype that can be assigned to the term *televangelist*. Not only are these women laughed at, but they give an already skeptical public another reason to doubt the authenticity of the preacher and his message.

It's easy to see how we as women can overindulge in our appearance. We live in a country with enough disposable income for a multi-billion-dollar beauty and fashion industry to thrive. There are specialty shops for women of all ages and sizes to find exactly the style of garment or beauty product they desire. There are magazines and blogs devoted to educating us on how to dress like celebrities. If we are inclined, we can even buy outfits for our dogs. In a society obsessed with designer handbags and shoes, it is easy for us to neglect certain scriptures which address our appearance.

While we are free to be consumers, we sin when we become consumed.

In like manner also, that the women adorn themselves in modest apparel, with propriety and moderation, not with braided hair or gold or pearls or costly clothing, but, which is proper for women professing godliness, with good works,
1 Timothy 2:8–11

While this passage in 1 Timothy uses the word *modest* when referring to apparel, it is interesting to note that the Greek word here is not a contrast to immodest. The word simply means "well-ordered and decorous,"[1] which goes along with the next part of the sentence, "teaching women to dress with propriety and moderation." Verse 9 instructs us to dress with proper decorum and moderation, and to refrain from showing off our finery, while verse 10 puts our appearance into perspective: we should remember to adorn ourselves with good works.

Similarly, a passage from 1 Peter teaches us what to emphasize when it comes to our appearance:

> *...Do not let your adornment be merely outward—*
> *arranging the hair, wearing gold, or putting on fine*
> *apparel— rather let it be the hidden person of the heart,*
> *with the incorruptible beauty of a gentle and quiet spirit,*
> *which is very precious in the sight of God,* 1 Peter 3:3–4.

When people look at us, can they see our good works? Are we known for our gentle and quiet spirit? Or is our outward appearance so distracting that people can't get past it? If our appearance shines so brightly that it overshadows the good deeds which are evidence of our faith, our mirror may be sending us a message about our hearts. We need to look within ourselves and determine the cause which is producing the symptoms.

Look in Your Heart:
Why Am I Dressing to Impress?

Am I dressing to impress the wrong audience?

Not only can we fall into the trap of dressing to impress others; we can also resent our brethren when we feel we are dressing a certain way just for their sakes. Colossians 3:23 reminds us, "*Whatever you do, do it heartily, as to the Lord and not to men.*" We must remember that the primary audience we are dressing for is the Lord. If we are first concerned with His desires for us, we will be dressed properly for every occasion.

Am I materialistic?

Many of us value stylish and high-quality garments, accessories, and beauty products. While we are free to be consumers, we sin when we become consumed. Placing too much value on material items causes our lives to revolve around them, Proverbs 23:7.

Soon our spirit is so devoted to possessions, there is no room left for proper devotion to God. When we are known more for the beauty of our clothing than for the beauty of our spirit, our heart is not prioritizing as it should.

Do I suffer from pride?

Pride develops when we receive a gift from God and abuse it. What a wonderful blessing to enjoy earthly wealth or physical beauty, but how disgraceful it would be to take those gifts and parade them before others in an unbecoming way. When we adopt the attitude, "If you've got it, flaunt it," we have pride in our hearts and bring shame on ourselves, Proverbs 11:2.

Have I forgotten what truly makes me beautiful?

Our physical bodies were hand-crafted by the same artist who designed waterfalls, mountaintops, and flowering meadows. Truly, we are *"fearfully and wonderfully made,"* Psalm 139:14. But as Samuel learned before anointing David king, *"the Lord does not see as man sees; for man looks at the outward appearance, but the Lord looks at the heart,"* 1 Samuel 16:7. God's desire is for us to cultivate our *"incorruptible beauty of a gentle and quiet spirit, which is very precious in the sight of God,"* 1 Peter 3:4. Our hearts should be most precious to us, as well.

Take a Look in the Mirror: Am I Immodest?

A woman dressed immodestly always stands out in a crowd. This is true even if the room is full of immodestly dressed women. While one might feel as if she is blending in, a low neckline, a short skirt, or a see-through dress will be noticed. There is simply no way to hide it. You can't cover up a body with clothes which aren't there.

As Christian women, we know we need to be concerned with immodesty. But too often we skim over Bible teachings about the subject

and reason that we merely need to *cover up enough*. Then, if we find ourselves second-guessing an outfit, or if someone has the nerve to tell us a
garment might be too revealing, we make excuses. We justify our right
to wear the item by thinking, "Those men should just get their mind out
of the gutters. This isn't nearly as bad as what most people are wearing.
These are the clothes available in stores right now. What do you expect
me to do?" We admit that we are not fully covered, but rationalize that
we are *covered up enough*.

Women have relied on their own wisdom to determine what is
decent and what is immodest from the beginning. When Eve and Adam
ate the forbidden fruit and realized they were naked, they sewed fig leaves
to create *coverings*, Genesis 3:7. However, when the Lord saw them, He
clothed them in animal skins, Genesis 3:21. Adam and Eve had made an
effort, but only God's involvement provided decent clothing for them.
We, too, must look to God's instruction on modesty, remembering, *"The
wisdom of this world is foolishness with God,"* 1 Corinthians 3:19.

Titus 2:4–5 is a passage which teaches women how to conduct
themselves, and it can be applied to our appearance.

> *[Older women] admonish the young women to love their*
> *husbands, to love their children, to be discreet, chaste,*
> *homemakers, good, obedient to their own husbands, that*
> *the word of God may not be blasphemed, Titus 2:4–5.*

A careful reading of these scriptures reveals two principles that
can be applied to our appearance. First, women should strive to be *discreet* and *chaste* (or pure) at all times, Titus 2:4. By striving for purity in
our attire, we will reflect a righteous woman, rather than one who is simply trying to *cover up enough*.

Secondly, failure to be discreet and chaste blasphemes God, Titus
2:5. None of us would dream of publicly taking the Lord's name in vain,

especially at a worship assembly or other gathering of Christians. But do we realize that we can be just as guilty of blasphemy by wearing an immodest dress, top, or skirt? We must understand that dressing immodestly has serious consequences. In order to purify our appearance, we should purify our hearts.

Look in Your Heart: Why Do I Struggle with Immodesty?

Am I seeking out sin?

> Consciously or not, some women seek out attention from men. They are flirtatious, emotionally intimate, and they wear provocative clothing around men other than their spouses. Even the way they carry themselves is inappropriately suggestive. When Paul listed the works of the flesh in Galatians 5:19, he mentioned uncleanness and lewdness among them. These words refer to sensual and sexual sins which are performed in an unflinchingly brazen manner.[2] Paul warns that those who practice these things will not inherit the kingdom of God, Galatians 5:21. A woman struggling with this sin will find help by studying the rest of this passage and focusing on bearing fruits of the Spirit, Galatians 5:22. The fruit of self-control can replace the fleshly work of lasciviousness.

Have I forgotten how to blush?

> When we become conformed to the world, rather than transformed by the Word, we may not even notice when we are dressed immodestly. The Lord once said of the Israelites, *"Were they ashamed when they had committed abomination? No! They were not at all ashamed, nor did they know how to blush...,"* Jeremiah 8:12. God's people were so far from Him that they did not recognize their own sins. Immodest dress is an indication to us, as well, that we are dangerously far from God.

Do I equate immodesty with ability to cause lust?

Immodesty is not entirely about lust. We've all seen overweight women wearing obscenely unflattering halter tops, bikinis, or short shorts. None of us thought to ourselves, "Oh, she must be very righteous, because she has dressed in such a way that no one will lust over her." Yet sometimes we fool ourselves into believing we can wear a shirt that has become too small by reasoning, "I'm so fat, old, ugly, or flat-chested that no one will lust over me. This shirt will be okay." Regardless whether it's attractive or not, dressing in an indiscreet and impure manner blasphemes God, Titus 2:5.

Am I simply careless?

A dress that hangs a certain way on your body in the dressing room won't hang the same way with a toddler sitting on your hip. A skirt that rests right at your knees becomes exponentially shorter as you sit down, cross your legs, and struggle with the previously mentioned toddler who is now climbing on your lap. The bust line on a shirt opens and drops when you lean forward. Nude undergarments do not show through white fabric, but white undergarments do. Dresses that look opaque in a dark bedroom can become see-through in the sunlight. Clothes are meant to move and function on our bodies, and when we try on an item, we need to consider its practicality. Carelessness to do so may be obvious only when it's too late.

Take a Look in the Mirror: Am I Underdressed?

While avoiding immodesty and decadence in our appearance, preachers' wives still have a responsibility to dress and present ourselves well. Much like wives of successful men in other fields, there are expectations placed upon us to present an attractive and pleasing public image. This sometimes comes as a surprise, and it can be difficult for any woman to face such pressure. Laura Bush wrote in her memoir, *Spoken from the Heart,* "I was amazed by the sheer number of designer clothes that I was expected to buy too, like the women before me, meet the fashion expectations for a First Lady. After our first year in the White House, our accountant said to George, 'It costs a lot to be president,' and he was referring mainly to my clothes. . ."[3]

Wives of successful men are often required to literally stand beside their husbands in public forums. While it may be the husband who is receiving an honor, giving a presentation, or representing a business, there are unwritten codes of conduct for their spouses. Wives are expected to look the part of a supportive partner—smiling adoringly, applauding if necessary, and displaying an attractive appearance. A man of stature needs his success reflected in his wife and children to maintain the respect of others. Apparent failings in his family life can distract from his professional achievements. By dressing as well as her husband dresses when standing beside him, a wife lends credibility to the message he needs to proclaim.

Wives have supported their husbands in this way throughout history. The Virtuous Woman of Proverbs 31 is so accomplished in her own right that it is easy to overlook one of her roles—the wife of a well-known and respected man. And in this position, her husband depended on her to help him, just as men of prominent stature do today.

Her husband is known in the gates,
when he sits among the elders of the land,
Proverbs 31:23.

The heart of her husband safely trusts her;
so he will have no lack of gain,
Proverbs 31:11.

There were many ways in which this virtuous wife brought honor to her husband and children. We can be assured that she was known by her heart and good works, because Proverbs 31:25 reads, *"strength and honor are her clothing."* However, her appearance was noticed by others as well, and we know specifically what types of clothing she wore. When referring to her garments, Proverbs 31:22 tells us, *"Her clothing is fine linen and purple."* The Proverbs 31 Woman strove for excellence in all things, including her appearance.

> *In order to purify our appearance, we should purify our hearts.*

Dressing well and taking proper care of your appearance not only demonstrates your support of your husband and investment in his profession, but it sends a message about Christianity, as well. When you are introduced as a Christian, or more specifically as a preacher's wife, your appearance makes the first impression people have of you. Have you ever brought a visitor to church and been concerned about the run-down appearance of the building? It is disheartening, because you wonder why your visitor would want to be part of a church which looks as if no one cares. Similarly, why would a person want to learn more about a faith in which the preacher's own wife looks as if she hasn't put any effort into attending the worship service? When we are sharing the gospel with others, we need to think about the wrapping of the gift. Do we look like a *"new creation,"* 2 Corinthians 5:17?

Look in Your Heart: Why Do I Neglect My Appearance?

Do I have a lack of respect for God?

We dress up for important events. We think nothing of looking our best for weddings, funerals, court appearances, and formal celebrations. We do this out of respect for others and honor for the occasion. Additionally, many of us dress up for everyday occurrences such as going to work. This is not necessarily done out of respect for others, but because we understand that we need to be taken seriously and thought well of. So, when it's time to get ready for a worship service, are we giving God the same consideration? Are we presenting our bodies as a living sacrifice, holy and acceptable to Him, Romans 12:1? If we routinely dress better for work and social events than for worship, we are failing to show our respect and love for our Creator.

Am I unaware that my appearance affects my marriage?

Regardless of your husband's profession, a man has a desire for an attractive spouse. As women, we sometimes fail to appreciate this because we view the world differently than men. But while we may get a thrill out of watching our husband unload the dishwasher, it means just as much to our husbands when we make a special effort to dress up and look nice. According to Dr. Willard Harley, author of *His Needs, Her Needs*, having an attractive spouse is one of the top five emotional needs of most men.[4] So, statistically speaking, there is a 40% chance that one of your husband's top two emotional needs in your marriage is for you to take care of your appearance. If at first, this sounds petty to us, we can simply remember how naturally this came when we were dating our husbands. Today, as well, looking our best is a healthy way to express our love and invest in our marriage.

Do I have a lack of respect for myself?

Maintaining an attractive appearance demonstrates more than a respect for others —it shows a respect for ourselves. We train our children to take care of their possessions and treat them with respect. We, too, have received an earthly body from God and need to take care of it. Perhaps we're so busy *"loving our neighbor,"* that we neglect to *"love ourselves,"* Luke 10:27. Or maybe some hindrance, such as poor self-esteem or depression, is inhibiting us from loving ourselves. Any of these problems are an indication that our life is not in balance. We may need to ask God, as well as those who love us, for help.

Am I unconcerned that I might be offending others?

The way we dress can offend the sensibilities of others. People have certain expectations of what a Christian should wear to worship services. These expectations change from one culture to another and even from congregation to congregation. For instance, slacks might be acceptable in one area of the country but not in another. While some women might wear jeans on a Wednesday night, the preacher's wife might turn heads if she attempted the same. Regardless of our own opinion of what is acceptable to wear to worship, we must think of our brethren and put their concerns above our own. We are not required to dress in order to please others, but we should make the same choice Paul made in 1 Corinthians 9:19–22, when he stated in part, *"I have made myself a servant to all, that I might win the more."*

Mirror, Mirror on the Wall, Am I Glorifying God with My Appearance?

Of all the expectations placed on preachers' wives, maintaining a suitable appearance may seem petty to some. However, given our public role, an improper appearance quickly becomes a distraction to others, at best; at worst, it is a stumbling block. While it is not always easy to find modest, appropriate, and affordable clothing, it is necessary in order to best serve God and others.

Ultimately, our bodies were given to us by God. They are not our own, nor are they controlled by others. Everything we have is God's, and when we consider our appearance, we should consider God first, dressing as a vessel worthy of the Holy Spirit.

Or do you not know that your body is the temple of the Holy Spirit who is in you, whom you have from God, and you are not your own? For you were bought at a price; therefore glorify God in your body and in your spirit, which are God's, 1 Corinthians 6:19–20.

Works Cited

[1] Reese, Gareth L., *New Testament Epistles: Timothy and Titus.* Moberly, Missouri: Scripture Exposition Books, 2007. p. 63.

[2] Wycliffe Bible Commentary. *PC Study Bible.* Biblesoft, 2003: Galatians 5:19.

[3] Bush, Laura. "The Private Life of Laura Bush." *Ladies' Home Journal* June 2010: 95.

[4] Harley, Willard F. Jr., *His Needs, Her Needs.* Grand Rapids, MI: Fleming H. Revell, 2001. p. 184.

Poll Results:
The Funniest Thing That Happened to Us Was . . .

THIS MAY NOT BE THE funniest but it has stuck in my mind. We were moving and we had a trash can that had seen its better days. We would be glad to have an excuse to get rid of it. In those days of just starting out and living off a preacher's salary, we hung on to all things until they were too sorry to admit we were the owners. Well, many came to help us and when we got to our destination, there was that old trash can again—full of trash! It goes to show your *trash* will always follow you around unless you come to Jesus.

∽∾

GETTING TICKLED IN CHURCH? YES, it happened. We were hired but hadn't moved to this city and decided to attend their gospel meeting since it was within driving distance. There was a good crowd and I was sitting with a friend, and my husband was sitting on the end, a few rows up with some others. A two year old got away from his mother and headed for the front, and she could do nothing but join in for the chase. He rounded the bend and started up the next aisle. Perhaps it was instinct—my husband saw him coming, stuck out his hand and never taking his eyes off the preacher, caught the little guy and held him until his mother could catch up. She was mortified and headed for the nursery. My tickles seemed to increase when I realized my friend was also tickled. I was furiously turning pages in my Bible, trying to regain composure, thinking all the while that people were observing the new preacher's wife!

∽∾

WE TOOK SOME TIME OFF to Gatlinburg and accidentally met some friends from church. At 3:00 AM we got a phone call that the brother from church had a heart attack. We went straight to the hospital and then drove to Knoxville. The next year, same date, we went to Gatlinburg again. Got a phone call at 5:30 AM. This same brother had died of a heart attack and the family needed us to come for the funeral. The next year . . . we went to Arizona for vacation.

WHILE WORKING WITH A CONGREGATION in a small western town, we met one of the sisters in town one day. While we were visiting on the sidewalk, she was holding her cigarette behind her back to hide it from us. Meanwhile, the smoke from the cigarette was billowing up behind her head. Don't know why she felt it necessary to hide her cigarette from us. God is the one she should have been concerned about and He is all knowing.

ON THE FIRST DAY OF a meeting, as I was sitting on the pew with my young child, a wasp landed on my shoulder. I panicked, being deathly afraid of wasps and whispered loudly to my husband to get it off—which he did by whacking me loudly with a song book! Then I had to take my child out and after a few steps my clothes caught the window blind and had to detangle before proceeding—not so gracefully—from the room. Singing there wasn't very good, so husband determined to sing out loudly during invitation song. It was one of those songs that fits two different titles so yes! He was singing quite loudly—only it was the wrong song. It was years before we were invited to return.

WHEN I WAS TEACHING FIFTH grade in public schools, I had a wonderful room mother who was Jewish. For our winter party, she asked if she could center the party on Hanukah to teach the children about Jewish heritage. I trusted her to expose the children to a different culture in a non-preachy way. The party was a huge success with her wonderful presentation; the children spinning dreidels, eating delicious latkes and applesauce and doing Hanukah crosswords while listening to traditional Jewish music. The children had a great time and I complimented her planning for the very successful winter party. I have no idea why, but in the conversation she said, "And so . . . what does your husband do?"

AS MY HUSBAND WAS PREACHING on the subject of the fires of hell, a bad storm came up. We were meeting in a basement building and water ran in on a circuit box and flames came out. A deacon's wife was in the room and came out running . . . and screaming. That finished his sermon for the evening and she has never forgotten the experience.

A WEEK OR SO BEFORE my husband was to arrive for a Gospel meeting, a skunk decided to take up residence in the basement of the building. Methods were sought to take care of the situation, including leaving the door open, hoping that the animal would leave on its own. That didn't work, so advice was given for another method that was tried. Method? If you shoot a skunk in the head, it will not stink. Wrong. . . . It gave new meaning to being a fragrance of Christ.

Money Problems?
—Change Them to Money Solutions—
by Dena Roberts

As the wife of a preacher, you and your family will be under scrutiny in many areas of your lives. Even if there are elders in your congregation, your husband and you are also leaders in the church and thus exert great influence on many people. Paul told Timothy in 1 Timothy 4:12, "*Let no one despise you for your youth, but set the believers an example in speech, in conduct, in love, in faith, in purity.*" As the "preacher's family" Christians will look to your husband, and you, as an example. One of the areas that people will be evaluating is your finances. If you and your family cannot be *faithful* with the money and resources the Lord has blessed you with, your sphere of influence will be greatly diminished and it will hurt the credibility of your husband as a preacher of the gospel. This ought to be more than enough motivation for any preacher's wife to want to help set her family on a course for good stewardship! We do that by making three key changes in our life.

Changing our Attitude toward this World's Goods: The Enemy of Materialism

John warns us "*Do not love the world or the things in the world. If anyone loves the world, the love of the Father is not in him. For all that is in the world—the desires of the flesh and the desires of the eyes and pride in possessions—is not from the Father but is from the world. And the world is passing away along with its desires, but whoever does the will of God abides forever,*" 1 John 2:15–17. John's words about pride in possessions and desires of the eyes really hits home.

Focusing on our heavenly home is the key to overcoming the desires of this world and self-discipline is essential in helping us control our material urges. This discipline does become easier as you grow older, however, whatever our age, we should be reminding ourselves of this passage every day.

Paul understood the problem of possessions and the desires of the eyes, and learned to be satisfied with his lot in life no matter what it was. *"For I have learned in whatever situation I am to be content. I know how to be brought low, and I know how to abound. In any and every circumstance, I have learned the secret of facing plenty and hunger, abundance and need,"* Philippians 4:11–12. Paul also refused to grumble and complain, Philippians 2:14.

Jesus reminds us of this as well. *"Take care, and be on your guard against all covetousness, for one's life does not consist in the abundance of his possessions,"* Luke 12:15. Covetousness is an inordinate desire for what we do not have. Jesus' words can be hard for us, especially when we see others with all the things that money can buy and the *fun* they are having, we seem to be missing. Of course, we do not always know if these people are in debt up to their eyeballs and have the constant worry about how they are going to pay their bills for all they have! Instead of focusing on momentary pleasures or material possessions, we need to remember what Paul said, *"Now there is great gain in godliness with contentment, for we brought nothing into the world, and we cannot take anything out of the world. But if we have food and clothing, with these we will be content. But those who desire to be rich fall into temptation, into a snare, into many senseless and harmful desires that plunge people into ruin and destruction. For the love of money is a root of all kinds of evils. It is through this craving that some have wandered away from the faith and pierced themselves with many pangs,"* 1 Timothy 6:6–10.

Let us make this very practical. What is your basic attitude toward your husband's salary? Many churches cannot pay high salaries. If you have to have the finest things in life, you will be miserable and so will your husband. This is a sacrifice that he makes and you make too for the cause of Christ. Then once you have decided that you are willing to make this sacrifice, don't be complaining about it all the time. Remember what Paul said about grumbling and complaining? If you are not happy with your husband's salary, don't go complaining to the other women from the church. When someone buys a new car, don't sigh heavily and say, "We'll never have anything like that on what we make." If you really don't have enough to make ends meet and plan for the future, then your husband should talk to the elders or men himself. Wives that are unhappy with their husband's salary in the secular world don't go talk to their husband's employer to get a raise! Spreading dissension and bitterness through the congregation isn't just inappropriate—it is wrong!

Many of these problems can be prevented if some research is done before your family moves to a new congregation. Find out the cost of living in the area so that when the topic of salary is brought up, you and your husband will be able to know if you can live on what is offered. You don't want to move to a place and realize that your husband is not being paid as much as you really need and then have to approach the elders or men right away for a raise. Not only will you look incompetent, but the church might not be able to support you at a higher level—and now everyone is in an unhappy predicament.

> *Most financial books begin (with planning) and budgets but the Bible begins (with our) attitude.*

Most financial books begin with planning and budgets but the Bible begins with our attitude. If our attitude is not right, nothing else will be. Once we have the right attitude and have put materialism aside, we can begin some of the practical disciplines, like budgeting.

Changing to a Financial Plan: Making a Budget

In every area of life, plans need to be made before beginning a project. Jesus tells us in Luke 14:28–30 *"For which of you, desiring to build a tower, does not first sit down and count the cost, whether he has enough to complete it? Otherwise, when he has laid a foundation and is not able to finish, all who see it begin to mock him."* Making a budget is simply counting the cost of your financial life. One writer says that "budgeting is telling your money where you want it to go rather than wondering where it went." The wise man says in Proverbs 27:23–24, *"Be diligent to know the state of your flocks, and attend to your herds; for riches are not forever, nor does a crown endure to all generations."* You cannot be financially responsible if you do not know the 'state of your flocks and herds.' A budget helps you keep track of what you have and what you owe.

When we were first married, I had never thought about a budget and didn't have a clue on how to begin the process. Now there are many ways to learn about budgeting, from books to websites. Let's spend a minute with the basics. A budget is simply a spending plan that looks carefully at the money you are now bringing in and then decides **ahead of time** how it will be spent.

To make a budget, you need to list every expense that you can possibly think of and write it on a sheet of paper. Remember, savings is an expense too, so think about the kind of savings that you would like to have. Other items that need to be included in the budget are giving to the Lord—first and foremost, not out of our leftovers—housing, clothing (your clothes do wear out), food, utilities, health and life insurance, gasoline, cell phones, taxes (estimated taxes are due quarterly), and books for your husband to study. You will also need to have a miscellaneous category for items that don't fit anywhere else and that occur unexpectedly. Make a budget for the year by writing down annual expenses (or estimated annual expenses) and then break it down into weekly amounts for each item.

Once you have this annual plan you will be able to see clearly how much money you need just to live, and how much money is left over for *discretionary spending*. That would include items we want but don't need—perhaps a vacation or new TV.

All you need to do now is keep track of the budget and spend only the allocated amounts for each expense. The easiest and most basic way to do that is with envelopes. You simply make an envelope for every expense and mark on the outside of the envelope how much money is to be placed in the envelope every pay period. Cash your husband's check and *pay* the envelope. This may seem tedious at first, but if you have never lived on a budget, it would be a good way to start one because it promotes an understanding of the process. So, if your budget calls for spending $100 per week on groceries, then on payday, you put $100 in the grocery envelope. When you go grocery shopping, help yourself to some grocery money from the grocery envelope. When the money is gone, it is gone. You must eat on what you have at home. You would do the same thing with gas, going out to eat, house payments, taxes, and every expenditure you make. Again, this system is very basic, but it works for many people because it keeps you from overspending.

Other people use an Excel workbook for their budget and they keep track of all money coming in and going out. Rather than using envelopes, they use an Excel workbook and then each sheet in the workbook would be a separate expense category that they put money into each week and take money spent out of. They balance the total of their Excel workbook with their current checkbook balance and that is how they keep track of how much has been spent on groceries, for example, for the week already and how much they have left to spend.

I was told of an elder and his wife that helped a young couple by telling them that they could have two bank accounts. One account was for expenses that are set (giving to the Lord, house payment, insurance, car payment, utilities, etc.) and another account was for expenses that vary. Then they put the money that they need each month in the set ac-count and the rest in the discretionary account. That way, they would always have the money for the bills when they came due. They also knew how much they had leftover for items that can be adjusted monthly.

Personally, we use the spreadsheet method. We have always been paid weekly, so every week we take the amount of money that we receive and allot the amount that we have decided on ahead of time to each ex-penditure that we have budgeted. Notice that I said *we*. The Bible speaks of being *one flesh* (Genesis 2:24), and that includes being one in dreams, goals, and plans. A budget needs to be decided on by the husband and the wife together. If one of you makes all the decisions, it will eventually lead to problems.

The Hard Part: Sticking to the Budget

Dave Ramsey, a popular radio financial advisor who has a respect for the Bible, says, "People need to act their wage." This means that you spend less than you make. This seems like an extremely simple idea, but of course, it isn't always as easy as it sounds. Credit and credit cards make it too easy these days to spend way more than you make. Proverbs 22:7 says, *"The rich rules over the poor, and the borrower is the slave of the lender."* If you get into debt by spending more than you make, then you are a slave to the ones you owe money to. Further, spending more than you make will cause you to be focused on your debt and all of the worries that go along with debt. This will be a distraction to the work of you and your husband for the Lord. Some, after getting into debt problems, even lose their integrity in order to make money to pay debts. If you are hav-ing a hard time sticking to the budget, here are some tips that may help.

Experts recommend that your house payment not exceed more than 25–28% of your income. A mistake that many young people make is that they buy a house when they are both working. With two incomes you can qualify for a very nice house. However, if the couple wants the wife to stay home when children come along, they should decide on the price of a house based on his income alone. Other experts recommend that your total income-to-debt ratio be no more than 36% of your annual income, so keep that in mind when buying a car or other large items. There is little argument that paying cash for everything as you go will keep you out of trouble.

An idea to make budgeting a little easier and keep hard feelings out of the marriage is to put into the budget an amount that each spouse can spend on whatever they would like. Even if it's only a small amount per year when you're struggling, it is extremely helpful. So, for example, your husband would have $50 per month to spend on whatever he is interested in and you would have $50 per month as well. This keeps couples from nitpicking each other over every single purchase. Another good idea is to designate a certain figure that you agree on that you need to discuss before spending. How much is just too much to spend, even if it is a great deal, without talking it over first? Set that figure. Also, be careful to avoid *revenge* buying. "He bought a new shotgun, so I'm going to go buy a new wardrobe." Besides being childish, this will really wreck havoc with your budget. You're a team. Act like one.

Saving

Saving is difficult for many people. However, this should be a line item on your budget. Proverbs 6:6–11 tells us that the ant prepares her bread in the summer and gathers her food in the harvest. She is planning ahead and we need to do the same. We need to be planning for short-term emergencies and also long-term retirement and possibly college expenses for our children.

Experts say that if you want to be financially secure, you need to have 3–6 months worth of expenses in the bank for emergencies. So, for example, if your monthly expenses that you must meet in order to live are $2,500, you should have anywhere from $7,500 to $15,000 in the bank just sitting there (making interest, of course) in case of emergency. Emergencies happen all the time. We are talking about car troubles, tires, appliances suddenly dying, a trip to the ER with the kids, or major medical expenses to name a few.

A budget helps us to prepare for the future. One area you might want to be saving for along the way is college expenses. Parents do not owe their children a paid college education. Many people have paid their own college education or a part of it. However, this may be something that you would like to be able to do. I would like to emphasize a point here. Many parents, when their children are ready to go to college, are primarily concerned about the money and costs. I suggest that we remember there are some things more important than money. Think about what kind of atmosphere your child will be immersed in if they go to the cheapest school you can find or if they attend a college just because they received a large scholarship or a full ride. Is there a strong church there? Will there be a strong network of Christian young people to encourage your child in the faith? Many children quit on the Lord when they go to college because of the atmosphere they are in or because the local church is not very vibrant and active. What is it worth to be able to save and pay for your child to go to a college or university where they can thrive spiritually? *Think about it!* If you are not able to save money to help your child go to college or are unable to pay all of it, that is something that you should start discussing with your child when they are young so that they have the option of saving for themselves. None of us want to be surprised with a large expense. Your child should be treated as you would want to be treated by telling them as far ahead as possible what their part of their education will be.

Savings also includes retirement. Most preachers do not receive pension plans. The sooner that you start to save for retirement, the better. There are many financial calculators available for free on the Internet that you can use in order to decide how much you should be saving. The younger you start saving, the less per month you have to save because the interest adds up. It's never too late to start though. Proverbs 13:11 says *"Wealth gained hastily will dwindle, but whoever gathers little by little will increase it."* Saving bit by bit will work in the long run. Don't fall for get-rich-quick schemes.

Credit Cards

Credit cards can be extremely convenient and easy to use, but they also can be very dangerous. Many financial advisors suggest not using credit cards. It is estimated that people spend more than they expected (more than they budgeted) when using credit cards, by as much as 15%. If you use credit cards, you should pay them off each month. If you cannot do that, the best thing to do would be to cut them up and use cash or your debit card.

What if You are Already in Debt?

If you're already in debt and aren't sure how to get out of it or just need some help, you need to find a plan that will work for you and get some counsel. Talk to other preachers who have their financial act together or to your elders. Seek help if you need it from an older Christian couple or from books or websites. Proverbs 15:22 says, *"Without counsel plans fail, but with many advisers they succeed."* Asking for help is wise so don't be afraid to ask. It's more embarrassing to end up in major financial trouble. Get help early if you need it. Don't wait till the house is burned down before calling the fire department.

Some resources that have been suggested are Dave Ramsey's *Total Money Makeover.* You can go to his website ***www.DaveRamsey.com*** to find out if he is in your local area, or to find a local station that carries his radio show. He considers himself a *spiritual* financial counselor, and while I would not agree with all he says about the church or salvation, he has a lot of good advice on money matters.

If your spending is out of control and you are deeply in debt, then cut up your credit cards and pay cash for everything you buy. Make a budget and stick to it. Then pay off your bills as fast as you can by cutting your budget to the basics. People have different approaches on deciding which bills to pay off first, so here are two methods to choose from. Some say to pay off your smallest bill first and then when it is paid off add that payment to the next bill and work on it. This approach helps people feel that they are making progress and it encourages them to continue. Others say to pay your loan with the highest interest rate first and then work down to the bill with the next smaller interest rate. Whichever you decide, make a plan that will work for you and do it. You have promised to pay for all the purchases you made when you signed the credit card bill or the loan agreement for your car and house. Now you must do as you said you would. It's the right thing to do. You cannot be the influence on the church (or your own family) that you would like to be if your financial life is out of order.

Change Your Spending Habits: Stretching your Dollars

There are various ways to help your dollars go further. Let me share a few tips with you.

Planning meals, cooking casseroles, and eating your leftovers will all help your grocery money buy more. Eating out is expensive and usually not very nutritious. I have found thrift bread stores where you can buy bread that is still fresh but may have an expiration date that is a little sooner than the bread at the grocery store, but it's about a dollar cheaper per loaf. Sometimes dollar stores or warehouse clubs such as Sam's or Costco can be a source for good deals. You have to watch and do the math to see if it's really cheaper than your local Wal-Mart. Pay attention to the tags on the shelves that will provide you with cents per ounce to truly comparison shop and get the size that is most economical. The larger items are usually cheaper per ounce, but not always. The grocery stores have sale flyers every week and items that are on sale are usually cheaper than Wal-Mart at that time. Don't be afraid to stock up on items that will last and that you use regularly. Our family likes to have breakfast for dinner sometimes. Eggs are extremely inexpensive and make a wonderful main dish along with pancakes and bacon. In the winter, we enjoy having grilled cheese and tomato soup for dinner once in a while. Both of these meals are fun, good for us, and very inexpensive. When eating out, split a meal between two people. Meals at restaurants these days are usually too many calories for one person anyway. Some families have had a "No Going out to Eat Month" so they can use the money for something else that the family would rather have or do. Drinking water rather than sodas or tea can also save quite a bit over the course of a year and it's much better for you and your family. I know of congregations where the families will pass along clothes to other families that

Stinginess is not what we want to pass on to our children.

have smaller children to help everyone out with clothing expenses. Keep passing it along and bless others with what you have been blessed with. When the girls were little and we went on vacation, we let them keep a notebook of money we had to spend to eat on the trip. We told them how much money we had to spend for each day. They were able to see that if one day we ate at McDonald's using the dollar menu, then the next day we could eat some place nicer. Another advantage to this was that they were making the decisions and we were not getting on to them about how much money they were spending on food. Share ideas with other moms and you'll be able to find what they are doing to be good stewards. In these times everyone is trying to be careful and thrifty.

The final piece of advice that I'd like to give is to not let money and finances be the main concern of your life. I'm sure you have run into people that are very cheap. Their first consideration for everything is money and costs. Sadly, this attitude is passed along to their children. We should be instilling in our children a sense of priorities, of using money wisely, and being unselfish with our finances as we assist the truly needy. Some of the most giving people that I know are people that don't have very much, but they are always willing to share with people who are in a worse situation than they are. *"Do not neglect to do good and to share what you have, for such sacrifices are pleasing to God,"* Hebrews 13:16. Stinginess is not what we want to pass on to our children. That could lead them to only be concerned with the here and now and making money over more important spiritual choices. Get your children involved in helping others; even if you don't have much. If you are financially blessed now or become so in the future, remember what the Scriptures teach.

> *As for the rich in this present age, charge them not to be haughty, nor to set their hopes on the uncertainty of riches, but on God, who richly provides us with everything to enjoy. They are to do good, to be rich in good works, to be generous and ready to share thus storing up treasure for themselves as a good foundation for the future, so that they may take hold of that which is truly life,* 1 Timothy 6:21.

With a few changes in our thinking and by planning, money can become something we don't have to worry about so we can be more active in the Kingdom. This way we can be a good influence and help to the people we work with in the local church. We want to be the kind of example that shows them the proper attitudes about money and how money can be handled by proper planning. May the Lord bless us as we follow His Word and thank Him for His blessings!

To Speak or Not to Speak!
—Holding Our Tongues—
by Betty Tope

*If anyone considers himself religious and yet does not
keep a tight rein on his tongue, he deceives himself and his
religion is worthless,* James 1:26. NIV

S o you've married your preacher . . . not just any preacher, but that special man who is your soul mate. Get ready for a wonderful journey through life! Though you may be naturally shy, you've already learned that part of this journey involves being a conversationalist. You've overcome that shyness to greet visitors at worship. You go around the church building and speak to each of the members at every service. You visit the sick, the lonely, and depressed. You talk on the phone. You exchange emails, text messages, and information on Facebook. No other generation has been blessed with so many ways to communicate. With every blessing, however, Satan has managed to turn it into an opportunity to sin.

Confidentiality

*When words are many, sin is not absent,
but he who holds his tongue is wise,* Proverbs 10:19, NIV

God's word is replete with admonitions about the use of our tongues. Just because we are married to a preacher, we are not exempt from these warnings. On the contrary, we must be all the more conscious of our responsibility to control our tongues. We are often privy to situations and conversations known only to our husbands. Untold harm can be done by sharing these confidences with others: Friendships can be irreparably broken; reputations ruined; the church divided.

Avoid the temptation to discuss problems with other members of the church. It is all too easy when in a social situation to reveal secrets just to have something to contribute to the conversation. Being able to reveal something no one else knows may even make you feel important and puffed up, thus being guilty of two sins: gossip and pride.

Avoid the temptation to discuss church problems in the presence of your children. *Little pitchers have big ears*, as the saying goes. Children may repeat what they overhear. Worse still, hearing about the failings of others may weaken a child's faith. More than one preacher's child has been driven from the church over church squabbles. When it does become necessary to talk to your children about the sins of others or problems among brethren, do so in a loving way, reminding them that people fail and fall short, but God's plan of salvation is perfect and the church is perfect as He designed it. When our son was a small boy, the greatest sin he could imagine was smoking cigarettes. On more than one occasion when he discovered a member of the church smoking, he would exclaim in his little outraged voice: "But I thought he was a Christian." Then I would gently explain that brother so-and-so **was** a Christian but he hadn't learned yet that he shouldn't smoke.

If you are outgoing and friendly, others will respond in kind.

Whether we like it or not, whether we feel prepared or not, sisters in the Lord may look up to us for wisdom and come to us for advice on all kinds of problems: marital problems, financial problems, health problems, problems with their children, problems with other members, or particular temptations they are wrestling with. It is our job to **listen** first and foremost. Some of these sisters don't want advice. They just need someone to talk to and pray with. They need to know you **care**. Give them a hug and the reassurance that they can get through this trial. Romans 8:28 is a good scripture to use for this: "*And we know that all things work together for good to those who love God, to those who are the called according to His purpose,*" NKJV.

Others **do** want advice on how to handle their difficult situation. It is always best to go directly to God's word. You might say, "Yes, this is a difficult situation you are faced with. Let's see what the Bible has to say about this." If you don't remember the passage you want to share with her, don't hesitate to let her know you will have to think about the problem and find the scriptures that pertain to her situation and then you will get back to her. **Be sure you do get back with her**. There may be times when you will want to share how you handled a similar situation, but make sure you back up your actions with Scripture.

Be prepared when your advice is not followed! Most Christians know the answer to their problem before they come to you. Some are not willing to follow God's word, either from a lack of faith, unwillingness to change habits and attitudes, etc. Be especially careful about meddling in marital squabbles. We learned to our sorrow, that after the couple has solved their differences, they frequently turn on the one whose advice they sought. Those who do heed your advice will have learned the correct way to solve their own problems by going to the word of God and how to comfort and encourage others dealing with similar trials.

Difficult Brethren

"*Reckless words pierce like a sword, but the tongue of the wise brings healing,*" Proverbs 12:18, NIV.

People being people, most every congregation will have at least one difficult member, at least one person who does not like the preacher. This person may have wanted some other preacher and thus resents the one the elders or brethren have chosen; or she really loved the former preacher and can't accept change. The disgruntled member will then look for faults in the preacher or his family. Since none of us are perfect, faults are easy to find. The preacher may be criticized for the way he dresses—

too dowdy, too flashy, too casual, too foreign. He may be criticized for the way he talks—southern/northern accent, too soft, too loud, or for some peculiar mannerism. Some criticize the way he shakes hands—too limp, too strong. The preacher may be accused of being too long-winded, too lazy, paid too much, not spending enough time in the office, spending too much time in the office and not visiting the sick (translation: not visiting **me**).

(In one of Jan Karon's books, her character is the new Episcopalian preacher, Father Tim. He comments that to hear some of the members talk about the merits of the former preacher; he must have worn a halo just walking to the grocery store. I always figured the author was either the daughter of a preacher or the wife of a preacher!)

This is a time for us wives to exercise loving patience and try to put ourselves in the shoes of the complainer. Our natural inclination as wives and mothers is to retaliate by lashing out and saying something spiteful in return. Now is the time to recall to ourselves 1 Corinthians 13:4–5:

> *"Love is **patient**, love is **kind** and is not jealous; love does not brag and is **not arrogant**, does **not act unbecomingly**; it does not seek its own, is **not provoked**, does **not take into account a wrong suffered**."* [Emphasis mine, BT]

Now is the time to be the helpmeet to our husbands that God intends. Ask yourself if any of the criticism of your husband or children is justified. If so, lovingly help him to make some changes. If your children lack discipline, make every effort to be more consistent. Be aware of where your children are and what they are doing. Have them sit with you during worship until they are old enough to behave, if allowed to sit with others. If you have teenagers, train them to sit up front where they will be examples to others and not be tempted to interact with their friends during worship. Teach them to turn cell phones off during worship times or leave them in the car. Teach them to be respectful of others and not inter-

rupt conversations, to not run in the church building, to wear appropriate clothing. Teach them about caring for others by taking them with you
to visit the sick, shut-ins, and to sing for brethren in retirement homes.
Teach them to prepare a meal, bake some cookies, or take a hand-made
garment when you visit to brighten up somebody's life. Even a flower
from the garden tells a shut-in that he or she is not forgotten.

Don't forget to include your children when you are having a
home Bible study with a prospective Christian. They need to learn how
to teach their friends the gospel and to have a ready answer when ques-
tioned about their faith. As they grow up observing their parents doing
good deeds and speaking words of wisdom and kindness, it will come
naturally to them to do the same.

Of course, if the criticism is of you, be honest and ask yourself if
the criticism is justified. If so, assure your critic you are making every effort to change. If appropriate, thank the sister for pointing this flaw out to
you.

> *So many problems can be solved if we just communicate with one another.*

How do you deal with
difficult people? We once had
an elderly sister who came infre-
quently because of her infirmities.
When she did manage to attend
worship she would sit in her pew
and inspect the women as they
came into the building to see if
they were wearing immodest apparel. I jokingly thought of her as *Inspec-
tor 12* after the old Fruit of the Loom commercial. How sad it was that
she couldn't enjoy her worship to God for being offended when people
didn't dress according to her standards of modesty. I am not saying standards of morality change with the years, but sometimes we can be too
critical of others. This could have been a situation that caused strife within the body of Christ, but we all loved our dear sister and exercised much

patience and restraint. Most of the time I couldn't tell you what someone else was wearing to worship. That is not my purpose in being there, nor should it be yours.

When members of a congregation practice love of the brethren on a regular basis, it is not difficult to make allowances for others and gently rebuke where necessary. As a rule, I believe the preacher's family sets the tone for this in a congregation. If you are outgoing and friendly, others will respond in kind. If you are not prickly and easily offended, others will learn to act likewise. If you let it be known that you will not listen to gossip, others will follow suit. Learn to genuinely love your brethren—all of them!

Not every question has to be answered: Ways to sidestep an issue

Sometimes you are asked questions that are better left unanswered. Even our Lord, during His time on earth, did not answer every question.

> Now when He came into the temple, the chief priests and the elders of the people confronted Him as He was teaching, and said, "By what authority are You doing these things? And who gave You this authority?" But Jesus answered and said to them, "I also will ask you one thing, which if you tell Me, I likewise will tell you by what authority I do these things: The baptism of John — where was it from? From heaven or from men?"
> And they reasoned among themselves, saying, "If we say, 'From heaven,' He will say to us, 'Why then did you not believe him?' But if we say, 'From men,' we fear the multitude, for all count John as a prophet." So they answered Jesus and said, "We do not know."

> *And He said to them, "Neither will I tell you by what authority I*
> *do these things,* Matthew 21:23–27; Mark 11:27–33; Luke 20: 1–8.
> NKJV

As we can see from these verses, Jesus sometimes answered a
question with another question. When a sister comes to you with a complaint about a remark another sister has made, you could ask her if she
has gone to the offending one and asked if she really meant to say thus
and so. So many problems can be solved if we just communicate with one
another.

> *And behold, a certain lawyer stood up and tested Him,*
> *saying, "Teacher, what shall I do to inherit eternal life?"*
> *He said to him, "What is written in the law? What is your*
> *reading of it?" So he answered and said, "You shall love*
> *the Lord your God with all your heart, with all your soul,*
> *with all your strength, and with all your mind,' and 'your*
> *neighbor as yourself.'" And He said to him, "You have an-*
> *swered rightly; do this and you will live,* Luke 10:25–28.

Jesus sometimes turned the question around and asked the questioner what his thoughts on the matter were. Sometimes it is helpful for
us to do the same. When the questioner wants to know the meaning of
a particular passage of Scripture, it is good to ask what her understanding of the verses is. Not only will that help you to understand her level of
Bible knowledge, but it will also reveal her reasons for asking the question. We frequently have brethren who will bring up a question in class,
not because they want to know the answer, but because they feel someone
else in the class needs the answer, and this leads to strife.

When you are asked what you would do in a particular situation or how you would handle a specific problem, you may want to give
a general answer. For example, if it is a problem about the conduct of the

spouse, you could turn to the Scripture to show her responsibility as a wife.

> *Wives, likewise, be submissive to your own husbands, that*
> *even if some do not obey the word, they, without a word,*
> *may be won by the conduct of their wives, when they ob-*
> *serve your chaste conduct accompanied by fear. Do not*
> *let your adornment be merely outward — arranging the*
> *hair, wearing gold, or putting on fine apparel — rather*
> *let it be the hidden person of the heart, with the incor-*
> *ruptible beauty of a gentle and quiet spirit, which is very*
> *precious in the sight of God. For in this manner, in former*
> *times, the holy women who trusted in God also adorned*
> *themselves, being submissive to their own husbands, as*
> *Sarah obeyed Abraham, calling him lord, whose daughters*
> *you are if you do good and are not afraid with any terror,*
> 1 Peter 3:1–6, NKJV.

We cannot control what others do and say, but we can control our own attitudes and actions, thereby possibly bringing about the desired changes in others.

There may be times when you are asked personal questions that you don't feel comfortable answering. These may be pertaining to finances: to how you spend your money, what bills you have, what you spend on groceries, clothing, etc. Or they may be questioning how your husband spends his time or even your relationship with your husband. You can smile and change the subject. Or you can make a joke and answer lightly, "I'm very sorry, I don't discuss that."

Occasionally brethren are very concerned that the preacher is living higher than they think he should. If someone comments on your nice home or automobile, you can say, "Yes, we've been very blessed." Don't make the mistake of always being on the defensive and feeling you have to explain what a bargain you got with every purchase you made. One place we lived there was a brother who always said as he left our home, "Come and see how us poor folks live." Meanwhile, if we were comparing possessions, which I wasn't, I'm sure he would have come out far ahead.

One of our dear sisters who is now retired, frequently mentions in Ladies' Bible class how she handled all the gossip in the office where she worked. When one of her co-workers would start in talking in a derogative way about another, or begin to use foul language, she would stop her and say, "I'm sorry but I can only listen to pretty things today." That stopped them in their tracks and worked without fail!

What if no one talks to you?

Then there is the opposite side of the coin. One complaint I hear over and over again from preacher's wives is that no one will talk to them. Keep in mind when you begin work with a new congregation that it usually takes time to make friends. People have their families and their circle of friends established. They don't automatically make room in their busy lives for you. Invite one or two families into your home on a Sunday evening. Your meal need not be elaborate: sandwiches and tea or coffee, biscuits and gravy or pancakes or waffles are quite adequate and usually enjoyed by all. Remember, it is not the food that is important so much as getting to know one another.

No two groups of people are alike. Some may have just gone through a division in the church. They are hurting. They are distrustful. You are a stranger to them. Be patient. Be kind. Be loving. In time they will lose their wariness when they realize they can trust you to keep a confidence, to be a friend.

Some people are intimidated by their perceived image of you. They may have come from a denominational background where preachers and their wives are put on a pedestal. In time they will learn that we are all brethren, each doing his or her best to serve the Lord. No one is perfect or deserving of the pedestal. The higher the pedestal, the greater the fall when our feet of clay become evident. Don't encourage this kind of worship.

> *The joys of our journey far, far outweigh the sorrows.*

Other brethren have been devastated when the preacher's family, whom they loved, moved away. In an effort to protect themselves from further hurt, they have vowed not to get close to another preacher or his family. You may have these feelings yourself, especially after a series of moves. Instead of dwelling on the negatives of moving around, dwell on the positives: you have beloved brethren around the country and sometimes around the world. You are abundantly blessed!

What can you do if all your efforts to reach out to your church family fails and you feel friendless and alone? Avoid the pity party at all cost! Reach out to others in the community. Join a class. It may be an art class, a garden club, a writing class at the community college. You will accomplish two purposes: you will be doing something to enrich your life and you will be meeting other women to whom you may be able to teach the gospel.

Finally, keep in mind that though being a preacher's wife entails some awesome responsibilities, it also brings with it untold blessings of God. We have the privilege of being married to a godly man to help us attain the goal of heaven. We are privileged to be surrounded by the best people on earth. The joys of our journey far, far outweigh the sorrows. *"Love . . . does not rejoice in unrighteousness, but rejoices with the truth; bears all things, believes all things, hopes all things, endures all things,"* 1 Corinthians 13:6–7, NASB.

Finding God's Direction and Purpose

—Leadership—

by Julie Adams

I heard recently that public speaking, public office, or that which puts one *out in front*, is one of mankind's greatest fears. We read about similar incidents of *inhibited* leading in Scripture.

> Moses said to the Lord, 'O Lord, I have never been eloquent, neither in the past nor since you have spoken to your servant. I am slow of speech and tongue.' The Lord said to him, 'Who gave man his mouth? Who makes him deaf or mute? Who gives him sight or makes him blind? Is it not I, the Lord? Now go; I will help you speak and will teach you what to say,' Exodus 4:10–14 NIV.

Do you ever feel like Moses? Better yet, have you convinced yourself that in **no way, shape, or fashion** can you be a leader? No matter where you are in life as the wife of a preacher, his position alone has *put you* in a position to lead. And while that may be uncomfortable for you, I believe it's imperative that we as preachers' wives step out of our comfort zone and lead **in some way, shape, or fashion**. I believe the Lord has said to you . . . "*Go, and I will help you!*"

My entire life has revolved around the work of a preacher. My father was Weldon Warnock, a gospel preacher. We moved and moved a lot. And we met wonderful people and attached ourselves to the hearts of many. Before I married, I had moved over twenty times! While I came to learn my role as the *PK* — preacher's kid, my new role started as the preacher's *wife* when I married Wilson. The old saying that you don't know about some things until you are right in the middle of them holds true with the life of the preacher's wife. I had a new role to learn.

In my career as an R.N., I employed managerial/leadership roles. With a bachelor's degree in health care administration, I have always enjoyed the challenge of vision and executing strategy. I loved seeing a plan going into action! Those positions also came with defeat and loneliness. To be successful and *sane*, I had to accept constructive criticism, but I also had to make decisions and direct when it wasn't the popular thing to do. And it could hurt sometimes. The same is true with being the preacher's wife and finding the leader within you. The congregation has called your husband (and you) to come be with them, become a part of them, and help them reach goals and potential in the community. So what is your responsibility in all of this? How far should you go in pursuing the role of a leader?

Leading by Example

Welcome to the *House of Glass!* It's uncomfortable in there isn't it? Well my friend, it goes with the *calling*. As hard as you try to immerse yourself in the congregation where no one sees you as the preacher's wife, it just *is* what it *is*…. **You** are in the spotlight. Some congregations are better than others at allowing you to be yourself, but at the end of the day, you are married to the most visible person on Sundays.

As a young wife, this is where you can shine. Although experience is not on your side, your life as a Christian must be your driving force to lead. It is difficult to be the *new* preacher's wife and to be *newly* married at the same time. And there will be plenty of people to suggest and give advice. But you can lead by:

1. Keeping your home.
2. Loving your husband.
3. Using language that is godly and pure.
4. Teaching a Bible class for children.

5. Helping a struggling mom who needs a break.
6. Taking a teenage girl out for lunch or showing up at her school activities.
7. Learning at this crucial time in your married life—how to keep your mouth shut. Learn it now, dear sister.

I want to elaborate on point #2 ... *Loving your husband.* Learn how to love your husband in the genesis of your marriage so that together you will be able to weather many storms. You will come to learn this life is not easy and, in fact, can be very lonely. There will be women who have not learned how to love their husband, who will find it comfortable to talk against him and their marriage. Recognize the warning signals of such behavior and do what you can to encourage godliness. But again, your greatest tool will be your example.

Growing in your marriage usually brings children into the picture. This can be an exciting time as I have yet to meet a group of sisters who didn't like giving a baby shower! When our youngest was born we had been with the congregation about a year. The group was made up of mainly older members and I had a houseful of excited *grandparents!* They were so very kind. In fact, on his first birthday ... the guests were all 55 and up! I share this with you to help with the transition of where your example will stretch even further. The spotlight that lit up your house with the two of you as a married couple now shines on you as a parent. Understand this at the onset ... you *will* make mistakes. And those who love you and may be critical made mistakes too. Be comfortable in establishing how you and your husband decide to parent. But please learn to listen to older women. That is one of the greatest examples of leading you can give to other women in your season of life. Scripture tells us that older women are to teach younger women, Titus 2. This has become lost in the last generation. Some is due to rebellion of those who have succumbed to the thinking of feminism, but some is due to the lack of leadership among older women. We have a *calling* here ladies, to train our young sisters.

Preacher's kids know the saying that the reason some of them have behavioral problems is because they have to be around the member's kids! Stepping into the role of parent while living in the *Glass House* has long been a source of contention. It is not easy trying to work so hard to live righteously without the finger being pointed. In fact, it is impossible. You and your husband must understand that. Follow Scripture when it comes to discipline and parenting for it is the best resource. I know there are multiple books written by spiritually minded people, but there is no greater book than the Bible when it comes to parenting. That is where you can lead.

As you begin to experience the *empty nest*, your plate may become fuller! There will be more opportunities to engage yourself in the lives of others. Experience is now *on* your side. Please don't neglect this season of life, as you will be needed. Sit down with your husband and discuss where you can help. Please do not initiate anything where your husband has no input. What you have in mind may not be helpful in his work. It may be that the timing is not right for different directions. But one thing that must be thought through is that you should not engage in any activity where people are purposefully eliminated or ignored or that it even appears that way. Philippians 2 presents us with how to imitate Christ and Paul instructs us to have the same *purpose*. In this context it applies to having the same *regard* for one another. The example of a seasoned wife practicing these principles may be met with resentment. But you have come to know storms and how the Lord has brought you through every one of them.

> *The congregation has called your husband (and you) to come be with them, become a part of them, and help them reach goals and potential in the community.*

Leading through Hospitality

I love setting a table. Presentation makes a statement! But that is not what hospitality is about. And I needed to learn to be Mary and *not* Martha. There have been times when I was caught up more with *meal preparation* rather than *mind preparation*. In Romans 12:13, Paul instructs every Christian to practice hospitality. And before that instruction he implores us to share with God's people who are in need. I don't think it's just me, but as God's people, the practice of hospitality has been overlooked, hidden, and blurred. Busyness along with multiple restaurants has gotten in the way of sharing our home. Many of you recall the days of Sunday dinner. Didn't you enjoy fellowship in the home of those who seemed to practice hospitality quite often? What happened? And what happened to just coming over for a cup of coffee or a glass of ice-tea?

What happened to you was probably what happened to me . . . I lost my focus. Is it really more blessed to give than to receive? Absolutely it is and one of the best ways to show that is by opening your home. And how does that work?

- ◆ Opening up your home puts your mind on others and off yourself.
- ◆ You will learn about other people and they will come to know you.
- ◆ Loneliness can take a back seat when the chairs in your home are filled with new friends.
- ◆ Your children will learn how to give of themselves by watching you.
- ◆ You will honor God through the practice of hospitality.

I know of a congregation where the preacher and his family never opened their home to others. And while the command is for everyone to be hospitable, this is where you lead. **Open your home**. You cannot go wrong with a $5 pizza and a two-liter. Why? Because your action says (1) I want to get to know you, (2) I care about who you are, and (3) I am taking the time to invest into your life.

The *preacher's house* is not as prevalent as it used to be. It usually sat close to the church building and you were quickly identified as the *preacher's family*. Unfortunately, many times the members saw that house as *their* house. In fact, I had someone tell me while still living with my parents in the preacher's house, that I could not put nails certain places in the wall. That type of attitude hinders hospitality. I would encourage, strongly encourage, members to allow the preacher and his family to make that house . . . *their* home. That family needs to feel that something is theirs. And, if at all possible, the preacher and his wife should be encouraged and financially provided toward the purchase of a house for that very reason.

Wilson and I started the practice of an open house where we invite the whole congregation for a come and go gathering. The response has been very favorable. The size of the congregation shouldn't matter. What you serve shouldn't matter. But your message will be that of openness and creating the sense of unity and oneness. **That** is what matters!

Why should you care? Because everything belongs to God. And without the Almighty you would be destitute. Your home needs to be a place where those who hurt can find solace in a kind word or a cup of cold water. You are richly blessed to be serving in the Kingdom. Show others the compassion that God has shown you. This is a priority for you as the wife of a preacher. Sounds old fashioned doesn't it? But it is just as real today as it was when Mary, who was with child, needed a place to stay. People have eternal value and the *stuff* you have cannot compare with the *stuff* that goes on in the hearts of so many. Whether you live in an apartment or a four-bedroom house, be content with what God has provided for you and learn to bloom where you are planted.

Leading through Teaching

As mentioned earlier, becoming part of a teaching program with the local work is important as a young Christian woman who is newly married and working to establish herself. With time, you may find it difficult as you move from place to place and learn how the teaching program is viewed. Some congregations put a lot of emphasis on it while others put little.

It will take about a year to learn the ropes of a congregation's teaching program. And by that I mean you will learn who does most of the work, who usually teaches, who won't teach, and how much money is allotted toward material. Some of those issues will be out of your jurisdiction. But you and your husband may want to introduce some different material and/or different approaches (I speak of nothing unscriptural).

> *Pray about it. Stay connected with those who encourage you. Be patient. Let God do His work.*

There are many more resources for Bible class material than there were twenty-five years ago. Some folks don't know that. And that may take some gentle persuasion and time. Some groups are on constant search for the latest *LifeWay* endorsement for Christian living. Yet that carries with it some dangerous territory in correctly dividing the Word.

Leading and teaching make up strong components of a preacher and his wife. Many times both are visionaries on what a congregation can become, its potential, and what tools are needed to facilitate that. Sometimes it is a sense of duty on how things ought to be and sometimes they see a "Holy Disconnect" in the congregation and cannot rest until it is addressed.

The greatest gift you can offer *leadership in teaching* is to assess the reality of the situation. What you think people may be ready for and what they are willing to do may be in opposite directions. You have invested your life into helping people grow spiritually. *(If this is not where you are as a preacher's wife . . . then I suggest you find the steps to get there)*. Your motivation may not be their motivation. They may be stuck in old ways, afraid of change, ego-driven, and trying to build their own kingdom. In your own setting you and your husband will need to seek and pray to find what is necessary for your group.

Once you have established yourself in a teaching role, it is imperative that people trust you. You must *walk the talk*. One of the greatest downfalls for your husband will be if you lose influence for the good of the gospel. Influence for good is just as powerful as influence for evil. Integrity will show when you are challenged. And for the purity of the Word to be upheld as well as the purity of the church, you must be cautious with actions. Isn't this true for any follower of Christ? Yes. But again you are married to the most visible person on Sundays.

These words especially hold true for women's Bible study classes. Quite often you will be asked to lead these groups. I've seen it over and over...the classes become an emotional purging for unhappy women. There's more *fluff* than facts. Pray about these situations. In James 3:1 we are told that those who teach will be judged more strictly. That makes me think about what I say and how it is perceived. Talk to your husband about it and learn to let go of something that must be handled by the men/elders.

I also want to encourage the *seasoned* wives to step out and write more for publications or be open to talking to women in a group setting. **I am not encouraging women to go outside of their God-given role.** What I am encouraging is those of us who have dealt with multiple issues in this life be willing to share the victories and defeats. Too often we search outside of known truth for something to feed our souls. I am all for reading the works of others to gather insight, but it is concerning that many gravitate toward a denominational endorsement instead of something written by one of our sisters in Christ. In fact, I heard one sister say that the young women would not come to a Bible class unless they studied a popular denominational women's author.

I believe with all my heart that many of us have much to share with other women where God is glorified and His word upheld. We have to get out of our *comfy cozies* and present it. You may not have the desire to write, but may I suggest you pray about it? You may not have the desire to speak in front of others, but may I suggest you pray about that also? The younger generation of women needs us to come forth with courage and compassion and share the blessings of life.

- ◆ Where else will they learn how to hold on to God's design for women unless they see in us the richness of such a calling?
- ◆ Where else will they learn how to "*be strong and courageous*" unless they hear from you that the battle belongs to the Lord?
- ◆ Where else will they learn how to depend on God until they see you rise out of the valley?

I heard a Life Coach say that one of the golden nuggets of a true leader is being able to *see* something that doesn't exist...*communicate* about it... and then *execute* the strategy to make it happen. Rise up to the calling my dear sisters! The responsibility is tremendous and the benefit is eternal.

Leading Alongside the Elders' Wives

Ever wish qualifications for the wife of a preacher existed as they do for the wife of an elder? Obviously that role is of great importance or the Lord would not have specifically taken note of them, 1 Timothy 3:11. One of the greatest blessings in my life as a preacher's wife has been the friendship and encouragement from elders' wives. And too, one of the greatest discouragements for me has been the discontent of elders' wives in their role.

I have been in congregations without elders. And in that setting, my husband has helped to lead the group toward getting elders since God wants His people to be led by shepherds. Sometimes ... people don't like to be led and would rather control (that's the sad reality). But for most of my life in the world of *preacher family*, I have come to love and respect the office of elders. And I have come to appreciate the *behind the scene* work of their wives.

There is one difference in our lives, however, that elders' wives need to understand. While *their* husband is a leader in the congregation, he also has work outside of this office or did at one time. His livelihood does not depend on those in the congregation, but mine does. I have always looked at my *bosses* in numbers. In other words, if the church has 150 people, then I have 150 bosses. And why do that? It keeps me accountable. And it enables me to be a more willing servant. It keeps me looking outward instead of inward. And the *reality* is ... their giving becomes our salary! They know what we make. In fact, it is printed monthly in a financial statement.

Much can be done for a local work when it is learned that we are all on the same team! A well-known leadership guru said, "Teamwork makes the dream work!" In order for the team to come together, they must learn to trust one another. They also have to think outside of themselves. And in so doing, believe the goal of the team is greater than the needs and wants of themselves.

Do you think maybe ... just maybe we could do a better job at that among the women? I do. And it starts with us as preachers' wives and elders' wives. Just like being *united* as parents shows *unity* to children, being *one* as women, **behind the scene**, shows *common purpose* and *love* for each other. Let's encourage one another toward a *team spirit* attitude.

Some of the most gifted women on earth are wives of elders. They are encouragers, lovers of hospitality, slow to speak, teachers, God-fearing, and seekers of good will toward all. Most of the time they have helped me find my place in the congregation. And they understand that I need to do that. They understand my role and help me not get trapped in the despair of loneliness—which is a very real world to many preachers' wives. "Thank you!" to the few who understand.

Leadership of Women from the Bible

Mary. I've wondered if I could have been chosen as the mother of Jesus. God must have seen something in Mary that demonstrated ability to lead by example. Scripture tells us she made a wise decision with Joseph as her future husband (Matthew 1:19 calls him a *righteous man*). And we know she kept herself pure for her husband. As a young bride, start your life with your husband with the example of purity and righteous decisions. With you by his side, he will be able to preach and teach the Word without worry. He will be uplifted and encouraged by your example.

Eve. Are you kidding—Eve? What could we ever learn from her example? I have come to admire this woman. She handled the *newness* of her life as it was given to her. She made the garden her home. She became the queen of that home. I cannot imagine the beauty of it considering who the Designer was! She loved her husband. She gave herself to him. She admitted her mistake and made the best of the consequences. She remained faithful to God and Adam. On the other hand, your garden home

Sometimes . . . people don't like to be led and would rather control (that's the sad reality).

may be less than desirable and…a long drive to the nearest Wal-Mart! This is where you learn to be content. I have not always done that. I've lost my focus. Remember you are a *helpmeet* to your husband. I understand there are situations that absolutely won't work, but if you can… find the "Jewel of the Nile" in your new location.

Esther. Ever had a "Royal Wake-up Call?" Esther did and she arose to the occasion. If we are not careful, we can become too comfortable in our surroundings to the point that our vision becomes blurred. God may put you in a place that will help you grow as a Christian and a leader. You and your husband are involved in fulfilling God's plan to proclaim the gospel. Sometimes the proclamation steps on hearts, sometimes people don't like what they hear, and sometimes you will be on the receiving end of the grumbling and complaining. Esther worked alongside the providence of God. She was patient and persistent. She knew how to keep quiet and she knew when to speak. That's a lesson for us. I can look back at many locations and see the providence of God was working. What I must do is learn that He still has plans for me. Perhaps you cannot see the good you are doing in the local congregation. Pray about it. Stay connected with those who encourage you. Be patient. Let God do His work.

The Proverbs 31 Woman. This woman had *noble* character. That means she had strength, skill, and was a warrior. This woman used the talents with which she was blessed. You have talents too. **Use them!** Leaders find their talents and focus on their strengths. Often, however, blind spots hinder leadership skills. For example, I like those small wide-angle mirrors that attach to the larger mirror on the car door. That smaller mirror is my reality check. It exposes my blind spots. Perhaps you need to broaden your field of vision and expose your hidden talents. For example, you may have great people skills that endear others to you, you may be a thinker that comes up with great ideas, or you may be able to take charge when things get chaotic. Whatever your strength, be the warrior God wants you to be in building up His kingdom. He still has more chapters in your story!

The Titus 2 Woman. This is the reverent woman who loved God. In the way she lived, she sought what was proper. Our culture appears to be unfamiliar with the word proper since it promotes *do your own thing, tolerance,* and *I don't have to answer to you!* Those are attitudes of rebellion. The Titus 2 woman did not seek to have her own way. The rule for her was to *do nothing* that would malign the word of God. Her mouth would not slander. Her influence was known for good. Look at what all she could do!

- **Teach what is good.** This woman knows what is in your best interest. She knows *good* because she is able to discern good from evil. Teaching you goodness may not always be pleasing to the ear. And this woman knows that. Her love for you will drive her to share what is true.
- **Train the younger women.** Being able to train means you have lived long enough to know what you are talking about. Your life is filled with mountaintop moments and heavy hardships. You *know* what it is like to lean on God for everything.
- **Train the women to love their husband.** That must mean she loves hers! If I am slandering my husband, then how could I train a young woman to love hers? You can't. This type of behavior will absolutely destroy the work of a preacher. Please take heed.
- **Train the women to love their children.** Women who have a heart for God will seek godly advice from older women. It's just that simple. And as older women it is our responsibility to do what we can to follow Scripture in the rearing of our families.
- **Train women to be self-controlled.** I cannot teach self-control if my attitude is *my way or the highway.* As an older woman in a leadership role, I must develop an attitude of humility. I must

have no selfish ambitions. I know when to keep my mouth quiet.

- **Train women to be pure.** Purity includes what I allow myself to put in my mind. If I am encouraging entertainment that promotes what God hates . . . I am not ready to train others. If I have a difficult time deciding what proper clothing to wear . . . I am not ready to train others. If I have language that would be embarrassing in public . . . I am not ready to train others.

- **Train women to be busy at home.** Your home speaks volumes about who you are. It is a reflection of what's inside your heart. We've had a tendency in the past several years to get our priorities out of sync when it comes to our home. The older women will train younger women to do their best to keep the home clean and with some order. They will teach them how to make a home that is welcoming. They will teach women how to be busy in their *own* home and not someone else's.

- **Train women how to be kind.** You would think that if a woman is in training on these other subjects that she would know how to be kind. The idea here is teaching how to go about *doing good.* This would involve teaching how to create an atmosphere that serves others. Goodness looks at how we treat our brothers and sisters in Christ. Goodness shows itself when we cross generational lines and reach out to older or younger women. Kindness is not self-serving.

- **Train how to be subject to their husband.** The older woman will help the younger woman understand this is *not* about equality but rather about headship. This is about *rank...*not rule. I've seen too many women who are bitter about their God-given role. Those women could not possibly train younger women while having that kind of attitude.

What great role models for leadership. The problem too often is that we are hesitant to take it on and follow what we have been told is our responsibility. It is not too late to start. The need is there. The calling is there. Now is the time to listen!

Find Your Voice of Leadership

In an interview with Tony Blair, Prime Minister of Great Britain, the question was asked of him as to what made great leaders. His response was simple. "A leader has to wake up every morning with a sense of purpose." As Christians we have a very strong sense of purpose . . . saving the lost! And as large as the responsibility of Tony Blair may be, it cannot compare with what we have been given to do. Sit down at your table with your husband and pray about this. Decide what you can do; what drives you. And then with clarity and purpose, embark on a *divine* mission to rise up and answer your spiritual calling. There is no greater time than now. And there is no greater purpose than serving our Lord Jesus Christ. Now . . . go take on the day!

How's Your Vertical?
—Personal Prayer and Bible Study—
by Karen Denhirst

*I*n a bulletin not long ago, there was some little one line sayings that really make you think. The one that you've probably heard in one form or another was, "Going to church no more makes you a Christian than going to McDonald's makes you a hamburger." You could say that, "Being a preacher's wife no more makes you have a faith of your own than watching the Food Network makes you a gourmet chef." Sometimes we preacher's wives can slip into being busy doing, inviting, taking meals, visiting, teaching Bible classes, and **being** the preacher's wife, that we begin to feel comfortable with the being and doing. That can become our *faith*. But we need to remember the vertical relationship we must have with Jesus, in addition to the horizontal relationships we have with one another. Our first responsibility concerning our faith is to **know** Jesus and to **know** His Word. Although our husbands spend much of their time in study of the Word and prayer, we won't have the vertical relationship as a result of just being his wife and being busy doing those things that show, even though they are important and necessary elements of our faith. We can't hope to stand on his faith; **we must have a faith of our own.**

Do we spend time, other than preparation for teaching Bible classes, studying, learning, and praying to strengthen the vertical relationship with Jesus that is the bedrock of our faith? If we don't know Jesus, the doing will be meaningless as far as our faith is concerned. Our doing only becomes important if it is the **result** of our personal relationship with Jesus and a natural reaction to that relationship. So how can we make sure that our personal faith grows? First, **we must make it a priority.** As women, we tend to let the needs of others crowd out some important personal needs. Knowing Jesus is the most important of those needs.

No matter what else is going on, we must make sure that we make time to study the Word and communicate with our God.

So let's consider the aspect of our communication with the Father, that is, prayer. Ask yourself, what kind of relationship would you have with your husband or best friend if your communication with them was equal to your communication with your heavenly Abba Father? Communication is an absolute necessity in having any relationship. Our communication with God can only come through spending time with Him in prayer and meditation. If you are like most of us, your day is already full before you even get out of bed. That may need changing. What does your day look like? Has your planning been out of order? How can you rearrange things so that your priority is your vertical relationship? Prayer connects us with our Father in the most personal way. Without a relationship with God, why would we expect or even want to spend eternity **with** Him?

Prayer is a spiritual exercise, a discipline in our lives. Prayer is something we must discipline ourselves to do. I walk every week day morning. At the beginning I had to make myself do it. I didn't even like doing it, but I knew it was *best* for me, so I made myself get out and walk. Now, there is really something missing in my day if I don't get my walk in. And most of the time, I enjoy it. It's really the same with prayer or study. Experts say it takes three weeks to form a habit. If we make a habit of spending time in prayer, we will soon come to need that time with our Father and we won't want our days to be without it. It *is* what is best for us. Ongoing contact with God will deepen our faith. In truth, faith and prayer are tied closely together. It is a very circular tie. Faith should create a desire to pray, prayer builds faith, and faith creates a deeper desire to pray and so on. So the point is we won't be able to have a strong faith without a strong prayer life. We can all gain the benefits of prayer simply by doing it.

Prayer is the voice of faith, and it will allow us to reach heights that we could not otherwise reach, and don't we really want to reach the highest of heights in our relationship with God? If our faith consists mostly in the things we do that are seen, our righteousness will not yield a heavenly reward, Matthew 6:1. We must truly believe in our hearts that, *"the effectual, fervent prayer of a righteous man can accomplish much,"* James 5:16. Remember the parable of the persistent widow (Luke 18) and the unrighteous judge? He changed his mind concerning her request **because of** her persistence. Look at the power of prayer! Imagine! The mind of the Creator of the universe can be changed by ardent prayer! Our Father wants us to come to Him with fervent persistence. We have so much to pray about and that demands that we spend much time in prayer. So, including having an ongoing attitude of prayer and praying throughout the day, we must plan for private time with God. Time in private, in our *closet* will be opportunity to pour out our hearts before our Father and will build and strengthen our relationship with Him in ways that nothing else can. *"But you, when you pray, go into your inner room, and when you have shut your door; pray to your Father who is in secret and your Father who sees in secret will repay you,"* Matthew 6:6 NASB. The Father desires that we bring our concerns and lay them before Him, and leave them there with surrender and trust. He will take our burdens from us if we will give them to Him knowing that His love for us is perfect and deeper than we can comprehend. He will always do what is best for us. How often do we find ourselves weighed down with burdens, asking ourselves why this or that? We don't have to struggle and feel defeated. We have the luxury of drawing to God with boldness or confidence in Him. *"Let us then with **confidence** draw near to the throne of grace, that we may receive mercy and find grace to help in time of need,"* Hebrews 4:16 ESV. Think of it — because of His spotless, sinless sacrifice, we can trust totally in His grace—**He is faithful!**

What a treasure we have in prayer! We **can** face the challenges of daily living through bringing our burdens to the One who is able **and** who is love. When we receive mercy and find grace by drawing near to His throne, we find the keys to life. The more we communicate with God, the more we'll appreciate and depend on his abiding presence. Our faith needs this time and the bottom line is — **our faith cannot survive** without the life-giving communication with our Father. It just makes sense. We can't expect to claim a real relationship with one with whom we don't regularly communicate. There isn't a time that suits everyone, but there is **some** time that we can plan for this necessary discipline. It must be a personal commitment. We must plan time to pray. Don't just sandwich this time in between other activities. Satan must be thrilled when we give God the left-overs. **He** especially knows that our faith will suffer, and eventually die without communication with the Father . . . without prayer. In the Scriptures, the message is unmistakable: "*Seek the Lord and His strength; Seek His face continually,*" 1 Chronicles 16:11 NASB. "*The sacrifice of the wicked is an abomination to the Lord, But the prayer of the upright is His delight,*" Proverbs 15:8 NASB. We see prayer as an integral part of the teaching of Jesus to His followers. "*And He told them a parable to the effect that they ought always to pray and not lose heart,*" Luke 18:1 ESV. Prayer was a natural reaction of the first Christians. "*And they were continually devoting themselves to the apostles' teaching and to fellowship, and to the breaking of bread and to prayer,*" Acts 2:42 NASB. The apostles left a clear message of their priority. "*But we will devote ourselves to prayer and to the ministry of the word,*" Acts 6:4 ESV. Paul encouraged and exhorted believers to focus on prayer so many times. I list just a few of those.

> *With all prayer and petition pray at all times in the Spirit,*
> *and with this in view, be on the alert with all perseverance*
> *and petition for all the saints . . . ,* Ephesians 6:18 NASB.

> *Continue steadfastly in prayer, being watchful in it with*
> *thanksgiving,* Colossians 4:2 ESV.

Finally, there is the example of our Jesus. The King of kings found it as necessary and natural as breathing while here on earth to spend time alone with the Father. Here are just a few examples:

And it was at this time that He went off to the mountain
to pray, and He spent the whole night in prayer to God,
Luke 6:12 NASB.

And after He had sent the multitudes away, He went
up to the mountain by Himself to pray; and went it was
evening, He was there alone, Matthew 14:23 NASB.

There are many other examples in Scripture, but even in examining these few, it can be obvious to us that prayer is not only honored by God, but we are commanded to enter into this personal communion and communication with Him. And what an indescribable gift we have been given in the privilege of prayer! We never have to make an appointment, go through assistants or secretaries, or wait until His schedule allows. No, our God invites us to come boldly into His presence and He hears us any time, day or night. How is it that in view of this wonderful expression of the Father's love and compassion, we many times simply neglect prayer?

We know that as preachers' wives we are sometimes burdened with what we view as more than our share of the difficulties of others. It is true that we are sometimes privy to many who need someone to listen, advise, or simply confide in. Others need us to pray with or for them concerning weaknesses or problems of a personal nature. Many times we end up knowing more than we wish we did because others feel comfortable coming to *the preacher's wife*. Although it is a privilege for us to serve others in this way, we can begin to understand the ideas in many religious circles that cause us to chuckle; you know, the idea of the preacher's wife being *co-pastor* with her husband, or the *pastor's wife* being in a position of leadership in the church, even the idea that she is somehow the *first lady of the church*, none of which are based in Scripture. However, we absolutely have responsibility in all kinds of situations and it is no different than anyone else's—to be there for them, and pray for them! On the other hand, we can also come to believe that we should have lives that are problem free simply because we are married to the preacher. That is perhaps the heaviest and most unrealistic burden that we intentionally or sub-conscientiously bear. How could you do anything any better for others or for yourself than to bring burdens before the great Healer?

A strong prayer life can bring about changes in our lives, and **believing** in the **power** of prayer will give us great peace. Prayer will cause our faith to increase. BUT, we have to do it. In 2 Chronicles 7:14 we see God's desire to hear His children as He pleads, *"if my people, called by my name, if they'll humble themselves and pray, and seek My face and turn from their wicked ways, then I will hear from heaven, will forgive their sin, and heal their land."* Before we leave the topic of prayer, consider the same exhortation that Paul gave to the Thessalonians, *"pray without ceasing,"* 1 Thessalonians 5:17. As some lyrics from a song by Steven Curtis Chapman say, "Let us pray without end, and when we've finished start again, like breathing out and breathing in, oh . . . let us pray." For you see, the truth is, if we're not doing it . . . we **don't** believe it.

Hopefully we see the necessity of a personal prayer life in our faith, but let's look at something equally important. How is your vertical relationship with Jehovah, Jesus, and the Holy Spirit through a devotion and study of the Scriptures? In your every day walk, as you interact with others, who do you want them to see? If we want them to see Jesus, which is who they should see, we must be filled with faith to the extent that it is evident that we house the Spirit of God within us. *"However, you are not in the flesh but in the Spirit, if indeed the Spirit of God dwells in you, But if anyone does not have the Spirit of Christ, he does not belong to Him,"* Romans 8:9 NAS. How do we get such a faith so as to have the Spirit living in us? The answer lies within His word. *"So faith comes from hearing, and hearing, from the word of Christ,"* Romans 10:17 NASB. Privately, in our heart of hearts can we truly claim to be in the Spirit or are we in truth, really in the flesh? I'm not talking about what everyone sees us do. I'm talking about what is **real**. In other words, what is my vertical relationship with God in the Spirit?

* *"But I say, walk by the Spirit . . ."* Galatians 5:16.
* *"But if you are led by the Spirit, you are not under the Law,"* Galatians 5:18.
* *"If we live by the Spirit, let us also walk by the Spirit,"* Galatians 5:25.

If we are expecting to be recipients of the marvelous grace of God Almighty as a result of doing good works, how are we different from the Pharisees? *"You have been severed from Christ, you who are seeking to be justified by works of Law; you have fallen from grace,"* Galatians 5:4 NAS. I know I can find myself applying this passage to others instead of seeing **myself** through the lens of Scripture. This kind of thinking usually creeps in when I find myself in a dry period, times when my personal prayer and study have been crowded out. My dear sister, if the only time we spend in His word is to prepare to teach or attend a class, we will not be equipped to walk, or live, in the Spirit. We may help others strengthen their vertical relationship with the Father through our teaching, but without personal meditation and time in His word, and applying its principles to **my** life, my vertical will be weak at best, and just possibly, dead. Remember how easily we can drift into **being** a preacher's wife in place of having a personal relationship with Jesus Christ? Do I let myself slide into thinking that being married to the preacher automatically puts me into a healthy vertical relationship with my God? Does what shows in my service to others or in my teaching become the only proof of my faith. Sometimes we get it exactly backwards. *"But they first gave themselves to the Lord and to us by the will of God,"* 2 Corinthians 8:5. The being and doing is important, but it cannot stand alone. It can't even stand first. What God wants to see in us is **life** by the Spirit. We can get by convincing others of our faith, but God sees the heart. What is truly in our hearts is what is honest. In our relationship with the Judge, the thing that matters most is the honest condition of the heart. Our vertical relationship with the Lord must exist first and aside from, what we do or to whom we are married. Am I saying that there are those of us who would actually say, "I have great faith simply because I'm busy doing a lot of serving" or "My relationship with the Jesus is strong, after all, I am married to a preacher"? No, even writing the words sounds pretty ridiculous. But we sometimes live as if we believe those ridiculous words. I know, because I have to guard against this lie to myself all the time. Let us keep honesty as an ever fresh ingredient to our vertical relationship with Jesus. In the end, what will matter is what Jesus meant to **me**. We must take to heart the advice we have heard and probably given. We will all stand before the Judge alone. At that time, we will be thankful for making communication with God and personal study of His word the priority.

I may be the picture of hospitality. My home may always be open and welcoming. Others may be drawn by my magnetic personality. My tongue may be hanging out as I endlessly serve others. I may even be one who does, does, does until I make myself sick. I could be and do all of these things and yet have an empty signal on my spirituality gauge. Everyone may be convinced that I am filled with genuine spirituality. But at some point truth will be revealed. If, in fact, my spirituality consists of all of this other *stuff*, not only will others eventually catch on to the truth, but more importantly my Lord will have known the truth all along. Glorifying Him through my life has at its foundation my honest heart condition. Jesus, after warning about the leaven of the Pharisees, *"which is hypocrisy"*, says, *"But there is nothing covered up that will not be revealed, and hidden that will not be known,"* Luke 12:2. In another

> *In your every day walk, as you interact with others, who do you want them to see?*

passage Simeon speaks to Mary, about her then infant son. *"Behold this child is appointed for the fall and rise of many in Israel and for a sign to be opposed . . . to the end that thoughts from many hearts may be revealed,"* Luke 2:34–35. If we keep in mind that the very thoughts of our hearts are known by Jesus because His sacrifice made personal faith and not merely law keeping the standard for justification, it will help us to make our vertical relationship the priority.

The thing is we have been delivered—**saved**! Now we must seek to grow in our knowledge of Him. If we really desire to walk and live in the Spirit, then we must cultivate the things of the Spirit, like the discipline of prayer and Bible study. In keeping these personal commitments, our vertical relationship will be constantly growing. When the vertical is healthy, the horizontal will naturally follow with the correct motive, to glorify the One who has saved **me**! Gratitude for what has been done for me will help to lead me to *"Be diligent (or study) to present yourself approved to God as a workman who does not need to be ashamed, handling accurately the word of truth,"* 2 Timothy 2:15. We can see from 2 Thessalonians 1:7, 8 that when the Lord returns He will deal out retribution to those who do not know God. To *know* here indicates to perceive or understand. *"But grow in the grace and knowledge of our Lord and Savior Jesus Christ. To Him be the glory, both now and to the day of eternity. Amen,"* 2 Peter 3:18. This requires planning time to spend in His word. I must constantly apply all diligence to add to my expanding faith **so that** I can cause Jesus to be glorified **now** with my life, not just by the doing, but rather by dying daily to the old life. If my doing is used to satisfy myself, I must die to that motive and rather do as a result of my knowledge of the need to glorify God in my life. Paul encourages the Thessalonians in his second letter to them, *"To this end also we pray for you always that our God may count you worthy of your calling, and fulfill every desire for goodness and the work of faith with power; in order that the name of our Lord Jesus may be glorified in you, and you in him, according to the grace of our God and the Lord Jesus Christ,"* 2 Thessalonians. 1:11–12. Jesus is to be glorified in me and I do that through knowing Him enough to be like Him. It is a serious commitment, not to be taken lightly. It is a battle that we are in, one in which we must, *"contend earnestly..."* Jude 3. We don't want to find ourselves as *cultural Christians*. What is that? A cultural Christian is one who is mostly concerned with playing the part, being accepted in the Christian culture. It doesn't take a deep knowledge of Scripture, just enough to *live the part*. Cultural Christians are interested in being comfortable in their lifestyle. We can become cultural Christians quite by accident. It happens when our forward movement in the growth of our knowledge and faith slows or even stops. We may get in the habit of still doing, going through the motions that satisfy us and feel comfortable, but those things alone will not grow and strengthen our priority relationship, the vertical relationship. So how important is this? Our spiritual life **depends** upon it. Yes, we can fool some of the people some of the time, but who cares about that!? If we are concerned about fooling anybody into thinking we are something when we aren't, then **we** are the fools.

A healthy fear of God is necessary if we are to have a strong vertical relationship with Him. *"The fear of the Lord is the beginning of wisdom; all those who practice it have a good understanding. His praise endures forever!"* Psalm 111:10 ESV. We want to gain wisdom and knowledge so that we can have confidence in gaining righteousness resulting in salvation. We also need to understand that our salvation will not be because of any party affiliation. The Pharisees felt as though they had taken out a patent on salvation. Membership in their sect was virtually tantamount to righteousness and eternal life. But of course, it was no such thing. God has never had a plan for group salvation. We are individually accountable to God and responsible for ourselves. Paul could not be saved by being a member of the Pharisees, and we cannot be saved simply by being members of a Church of Christ. We **can** and **will** be saved through our faith in the blood of Jesus Christ.

Scripture makes it clear that Christians need the fellowship of local churches; we are to *"stir one another up to love and good works,"* Hebrews 10:24 ESV. A solid church family is critical to spiritual growth. But we are not saved by belonging to a local church; we're saved by belonging to the Lord Jesus Christ. First and foremost we belong to Jesus, and only in Him do we have righteousness.

Sometimes we act as if rebellion against God only means things like a failure to attend services, committing adultery, being a drug addict or criminal, etc. — or rebellion in our minds may only describe one who is a complete reprobate. Isaiah 50:5 says, *"The Sovereign Lord has opened my ears, and I have not been rebellious; I have not drawn back,"* NIV. It seems from this verse that rebellion is identified as not drawing back from what my ears have been opened to—His word. So is it possible that a scriptural definition of rebellion could be drawing back from the Word of our God? We can attend church at every service week after week, stay busy seeing to everyone's needs, taking, doing, teaching, being… and still rebel against God. If we continue to seek answers and satisfaction

> *When the vertical is healthy, the horizontal will naturally follow with the correct motive.*

in something other than God's word, and are not taking the study of it seriously, we are in a state of rebellion. Psalm 107:10–21 is not reflective of the suffering and healing of physical illness. No, here God sent His Word to heal a much more serious illness, rebellion against Him and refusal to accept the counsel of His will. In their attempt to be free from His authority, God's people became prisoners in iron chains. Verse 20 makes such an important statement. *"He sent out His word and healed them, and delivered them from their destruction,"* ESV. What we see here is that God's Word is His primary healing agent. His people were in bondage because they rebelled against Him and turned away from His counsel. They were suffering because they lacked God's Word. The Word was the only thing that could heal them. Many of us are in such great need of the healing power of God's wonderful Word, and yet we choose to lay it aside and not dedicate time and effort to studying the healing answer. The Bible is the written Word that reveals to us the living Word Who is able to heal and deliver us.

We need to develop a true love for the Word; we need to pray for Him to help us develop this love. It's time to quit wrestling with the burdens and accept the cure for what is our most serious illness—spiritual illness. All of the answers are in His Word. He loves us so much. It is time that we fall completely in love with Jesus. If that phrase makes you uncomfortable, perhaps you should examine why that is. Without apology, I say it again; **it's time to fall completely in love with Jesus.** Love and gratitude will steer us to the healing Word. Our love and gratitude will be demonstrated in the importance we place on strengthening our most precious vertical relationship. Do it! Make the time to devote yourself to learning, stretching, and growing. Hide it in your heart, commit it to memory. Re-examine principles anew as you grow; as you do, you will expand your understanding about many things. Growth just isn't defined as busyness. Sometimes we need to do as this passage says, *"Be still, and know that I am God,"* Psalm 46:10 ESV. Meditate on the treasure of His Word! Feel the comfort and excitement contained in this never ending story. Lose **yourself** in the beauty of surrender. Now **that** is freedom! You can't really live without a priority relationship with the Lord.

Do you want to be of the greatest aid and encouragement to your husband, the preacher? Love your man, be a servant, be willing to take your place in the church family, but, most of all, have a strong personal relationship with your God. Only then can you be the most suitable help to your husband, because only then can you really help him get to heaven. Who knows him better? Who has the best opportunity to help him overcome his struggles through the healing Word? **You** do. As you walk this road together with the view of heaven right over the horizon, show him the greatest love of all. Show him that you have given your life up for a relationship with the Lord.

O God, you are my God, earnestly I seek you; my soul
thirsts for you; my flesh faints for you, as in a dry and
weary land where there is no water. So I have looked upon
you in the sanctuary, beholding your power and glory.
Because your steadfast love is better than life, my lips will
praise you. So I will bless you as long as I live: in your
name I will lift up my hands, Psalm 63:1–3 ESV.

Are personal prayer and Bible study important? Even more than important, they are life.

So, let me ask you, "How's your vertical, preacher's wife?"

Fellow Workers in the Kingdom
—Soul Winning—
by Cheryl Robertson

There is no greater role a preacher's wife can play in her husband's job than to support his efforts to seek and save the lost. The greatest joy a Christian can experience is leading, teaching, and encouraging a lost soul to know Christ and make the commitment to follow Him (3 John 4); however, evangelism is sometimes our greatest weakness. It is something we know we should do, ought to do, but fail to do. It may be awkward, inconvenient, and difficult. It requires patience and self-sacrifice. It means working with people and all the baggage of life that they bring with them. Yet if our efforts help teach a lost soul, turn an erring Christian back to the Lord, or encourage a weak brother or sister to persevere, how can we not get involved?

The Bible gives us no example of a *preacher's wife*; however, God does give us some brief insights into the lives of Priscilla and Aquila, a married couple who were major influences not only in the lives of two of the greatest New Testament preachers, Paul and Apollos, but also in the work of several New Testament churches, Corinth, Ephesus, and Rome. What did they do?

- Showed hospitality to Paul in Corinth, Acts 18:3
- Worked as tentmakers with Paul, Acts 18:3
- Taught Apollos about the life, death, and resurrection of Christ, Acts 18:26
- Hosted the churches of Ephesus and Rome in their house, 1 Corinthians 16:19; Romans 16:5
- Risked their lives for Paul's sake, Romans 16:4
- Were greeted by Paul as fellow workers, Romans 16:3

Evangelism is not a program or a checklist. It is not about a certain procedure or process. An evangelistic spirit encompasses all that we are and every aspect of our lives. It is seeing every person as a soul with an eternal destiny. What can I do to turn them toward heaven? How do I need to prepare my heart to be more evangelistic and help my husband in his teaching endeavors? Let us take a look at the life of Priscilla to learn how we can develop a stronger evangelistic spirit.

Priscilla had knowledge of the Scriptures and used this knowledge to teach others.

When Priscilla and Aquila heard Apollos, they realized he was teaching the truth, yet they also recognized he was not presenting the entire truth. His teaching stopped with the baptism of John. They took him aside and *"explained to him the way of God more accurately,"* Acts 18:26. We may assume they were Christians when they met Paul in Corinth, but there is no doubt that the time the apostle Paul spent in their home prepared this couple for teaching and serving others.

We too must know the Word. We cannot teach what we do not know. We must spend time in the Scriptures to deepen our own personal faith as well as to prepare ourselves to teach and serve others.

As the preacher's wife, there will be many opportunities to teach. Some, such as private studies that may come from visitors, community outreach programs, or members asking you to study with their family or friends, will present themselves because of the preacher's job. Some may come from our personal outreach effort in identifying friends or neighbors that have not heard the gospel. Some may involve public teaching such as leading a ladies' Bible class or a children's class. Regardless of the type, we must prepare our hearts to accept these opportunities and make sure we continue to deepen our knowledge of Scripture and grow in our personal relationship with Christ so we can readily take on these situations as they present themselves. Priscilla and Aquila did not wait for someone else to do it. They took the initiative and taught Apollos, who in turn taught many more people about Christ.

Priscilla was hospitable.

Not only did Paul live with Priscilla and Aquila while in Corinth, they hosted the church in their home while living in Ephesus and Rome, Acts 18:3; 1 Corinthians 16:19; Romans 16:5.

Hospitality, despite being a command (Romans 12:13), is becoming a lost art. We are too busy. Our homes are too messy. Our lives are too compartmentalized. We do not have time for hospitality. When was the last time you hosted a Bible class, individual or group? Allowed someone to stay in your home? Shared your table with a new convert or newcomer to the congregation? Invited someone over who was not a part of your inner circle of friends?

Hospitality can be defined as the reception and entertainment of strangers. Obviously, in our society, you should use common sense regarding safety before inviting someone into your home, especially if children are present. Yet once this is established, failing to use our homes which are blessings from God to further His kingdom, shows poor stewardship on our part. We can use our homes to teach people the gospel and to edify and encourage other Christians.

While my husband was participating in a young preacher's training program, it was a requirement that he live with the family of each elder for approximately six weeks. He observed how other homes operated differently from his own. He had many conversations with the elder and his wife that would not have occurred in the office or in the church aisles. He saw how hard they worked in serving the congregation and many of the *behind the scene* activities that occupied their time. He saw how valuable the elder's wife was in the execution of his duties. Through this more intimate portion of the program, he learned people skills that have served him well during his own years of preaching as well as lessons he has brought into our marriage.

After the six months or so of rotating among the elders, he was allowed to make his own decision about housing. Another family invited him to live with them. They had hosted the previous trainee, and it had been a valuable experience for them, especially for their high school age son. Words cannot describe the gratitude and love we feel for this family. Their generosity with their home, their time, their wisdom, and their love has extended far beyond the eighteen months he lived with them. When we married, they continued to have us over for meals, to play games, to visit, and to teach through word and example. We have laughed together, vacationed together, and even cried together when that family was devastated by cancer. This rich relationship that has affected our lives positively for more than twenty years began with an offer of hospitality.

A couple of years ago, it was our turn to pay it forward. A young man was interested in a summer preacher training program and the elders of our congregation decided to offer one. We asked him to live with us for the summer. Since he was converted during college, this gave him the opportunity not only to observe a Christian family but also the preacher's family. I trust that the time he spent with us proved valuable in his growth as a Christian and as a young gospel preacher. It certainly benefited our lives and enhanced the lives of our children. Even though we now live in completely different areas of the country, we anticipate hearing good things from his future work in the kingdom and we are happy to have been a small part in his spiritual development.

In Titus 2:4–5, older women are told to "*admonish the young women to love their husbands, to love their children, to be discreet, chaste, homemakers, good, obedient to their own husbands, that the word of God may not be blasphemed.*" Although these lessons may be taught during a public class, it has been my experience that they are best learned in more informal settings and are best received when given by an older woman who has shown love and concern for the younger woman through the development of relationships. We once had a young single Christian lady stay with us for a few days following some health problems and difficult life circumstances. When I invited her, I thought that some balanced meals, adequate sleep, and companionship would be beneficial. After a day or two, she remarked how lucky our children were to have Christian parents and to be raised in a Christian home. She did not have this *basic luxury* that many of us have taken for granted. I realized this was her first experience in observing daily living in a Christian household. Even though she had been to our house several times and we had had multiple conversations, this added another level of depth to her knowledge. I pray it gave her insight to choose a godly man for a spouse and to have a determination to rear their children in the Lord. We need to be mindful that many young women who are converted to the Lord may have come from broken homes, may have no parenting training, or may have few basic homemaking skills. By taking an interest in them and showing them how to be godly wives and mothers through our active words of teaching and our examples of implementation, we can help shape future generations.

Hospitality should extend beyond our homes. At the worship services, we need to greet our visitors with a warm, sincere welcome. A friend of mine worked by long distance phone calls and e-mails for approximately four years to teach the gospel to a co-worker in another city. When she was ready to be baptized, my friend referred her to a local congregation. When that co-worker attended the service, the members were neither friendly nor welcoming so she chose to attend another congregation. Obviously, this was very frustrating to my friend. Why would anyone want to attend a church where they were not wanted? How can we ignore someone when they come in the door yet expect to stir them to love and good works, Hebrews 10:24? Until you greet these visitors with a welcoming smile and get to know something about them, you do not know if they are strong Christians passing through the area or if they live

Evangelism is not a program or a checklist.

three doors down the street and have a desire to change their lives.

The *greeting visitors* task may be assigned to one or more deacons. That is good for them to be responsible for obtaining visitor cards and addressing any other possible needs. As women, however, we should also make sure we welcome the visitors, especially other women. I usually scan the auditorium when I arrive and try to meet as many newcomers as I can on the way to my seat. Then as soon as the service is over, I make my way around to the ones I missed. When my children were smaller (older preschool/young elementary ages), this presented a problem. How could I supervise my children after church services and also greet the visitors or other members? We made a *deal* with our kids—they had to stay on *our* pew after all three services and if they obeyed, we stopped for ice cream on Wednesday nights. They could talk, play, or walk around but they had to stay on *our* bench. I could easily scan the auditorium and see where they were and if they were behaving. It is true that we had some people who thought this was *cruel and unusual punishment*. I do not usually advocate food as treats, but this was a win/win for us. I had the peace of mind that my children were not running around the building or getting into mischief. They received ice cream. There were very few weeks that we missed an ice cream treat.

Sometimes, hospitality is easier than at other times. It helps if you have basic cleaning routines and menus. There are many books devoted to these topics. The main thing is to be yourself. Hospitality is not just about sharing your *stuff*. It is about sharing yourself and sharing the grace of God and the love of Christ. It is about making the other person feel comfortable and relaxed. It is showing them they are important both to God and to you. In addition, your life will be enriched by sharing it with others.

Priscilla did not allow secular responsibilities to hinder her from fulfilling her spiritual duties.

Priscilla worked as a tentmaker with her husband, and yet she is also considered a fellow worker in Christ Jesus, Acts 18:3; Romans 16:3. Likewise, our secular obligations or interests present us with more opportunities to reach out to the lost. How can we be a light to the world if we stay in our homes and church buildings? Getting out into the community is the way we meet people and establish relationships. It is a means to get dialogue started. We get to know other mothers at library story time, the playground, or in preschool groups. We can make a difference by participating in the PTA or by volunteering in our children's schools. We can influence other families by taking part in community sports leagues. We can interact with medical workers and home care personnel through caring for aged parents. We can affect positively the lives of co-workers as we interact with them on a daily basis. We can meet our neighbors through block parties or by walking the neighborhood. We can volunteer with Meals on Wheels, the Red Cross, or other service-oriented agencies. The list is endless. If we want to influence people for Christ, we must get out there and let them see Christ in us. We cannot wait for people to drive by the church building, see the sign, and walk in the door. We must invite.

How can we be a light to the world if we stay in our homes and church buildings?

New to town, my neighbor and I were discussing our lack of friends. I remarked that I did not know many people except people at church and she was welcome to come with me at any time. Nothing happened for quite a while. We continued to visit in the afternoons and let the kids play in the yard after naps. Several months later, I passed out flyers for our upcoming gospel meeting. She came! This began many weeks of home Bible discussions as she continued to attend worship services. Her husband worked out of town. Eventually, they moved to another state. They found a church there and the elderly preacher continued to study with them. I am thrilled to say that they are now both strong Christians, her husband is beginning to preach on a regular basis, and her children are being reared in the Lord. This was a long process but it began from a simple invitation between two young mothers with young children seeking friendships. In whatever season your life may be, use your secular obligations to create spiritual opportunities.

Priscilla was a risk taker.

We are not told of the details but Paul thanks Priscilla and Aquila for risking their necks for his life, Romans 6:4. Although it may be doubtful we will have to risk our lives for the gospel, we do have to get out of our comfort zones. We do have to risk our need for approval. We may have to stretch ourselves out of our basic personality traits. We may have to overcome shyness. We may have to learn to be more outgoing and reach out to others. We may need to become a better public speaker or Bible student to teach ladies' classes. We may have to develop courage to invite someone to services or to have a Bible study. Paul says, "*I have become all things to all men, that I might by all means save some,*" 1 Corinthians 9:22b. It could not have been easy for Priscilla and Aquila to approach Apollos, an eloquent and powerful teacher. Yet they did. He accepted the truth. Many souls were saved as a result of their willingness to take a risk.

Priscilla was Aquila's helpmeet.

Priscilla and Aquila are mentioned six times in the New Testament and each time they are mentioned together as a couple, Acts 18:2, 18, 26; Romans 16:3–5; 1 Corinthians 16:19; 2 Timothy 4:19. Paul called them his *fellow workers.*

A friend once gave me the following advice: "You are not 'the preacher's wife', you are Phil's wife. Do whatever he needs you to do." This advice has kept me balanced whenever I feel the pressure of "What do people at church expect of me?" I ask myself, "What does God expect me to do or to be? What does my husband expect me to do or to be?"

Sometimes he needs me to go with him to a study. Sometimes he needs me to have the study or visit in our home so I need to make sure the house is presentable or the meal prepared. Sometimes he needs me to take care of things at home with the kids while he is out of town. Sometimes I must rearrange my schedule to accommodate his. I should do whatever he needs at that time to support his evangelistic efforts.

The New Testament does not mention if Aquila and Priscilla had children so I would assume they did not. However, a study on wives and evangelism would be incomplete if I did not add that your most precious evangelistic opportunities ride around in the back of your minivan every day. What are you teaching them by word and example?

First, make sure you are teaching them the Word of God. Fathers are commanded to *"bring them up in the training and admonition of the Lord,"* Ephesians 6:4. Whereas this task should not be delegated to the mother, she does have many opportunities to assist her husband in this endeavor. Do not depend on the Bible class program where you worship to adequately teach and train your children. The quality of the program may vary because of the size of the congregation, curriculum choices, teacher preparation, parental involvement, or number of children in the congregation. As the preacher's wife, you may be very involved with the development and implementation of the Bible class program. Your program may be excellent, but it is limited in what can be accomplished in two hours per week. In addition, your child may be completing a study, for example the Old Testament, and your husband changes jobs. You move to another congregation, and the child starts over again in the Old Testament. When is he going to study the life of Christ? Our congregation has a great Bible class program; however, we have chosen another curriculum to use at home in addition to the lessons the children have in Bible class. The other day, as we ended the story of Abimelech, the self-appointed judge, our son asked, "Can we act this out?" Out came the props and the scene concluded with his sister standing on the arm of the couch and dropping a pillow on his head. He fell to the ground and begged someone to kill him so he would not be killed by a woman! Do not miss the fun of teaching God's Word to your children. Do not miss the joy as His Word penetrates their hearts and lives.

> *They must do their Bible lessons and know Bible answers because they are Phil & Cheryl's kids . . .*

Secondly, what are you teaching your children by example? We certainly do not want our children to grow up and say that they will never be a preacher or a preacher's wife or even worse a Christian because of the hardships they may have seen us face. Do they see you serving others out of obligation or out of love and concern? Do they see you going about your activities as a martyr, i.e., "We have to do it because Dad is the preacher"? Our children are now old enough to ask, "Why do we have to do it when no one else does?" This usually is not true. Many others are very active in His service; our children are just not yet old enough to see the big picture. However, we try to respond that this is what God expects of us as Christians, not because Dad is the preacher. We must do what God wants us to do—visit the sick, give rides to services, attend funerals, take food to others, and many other activities of service. They must do their Bible lessons and know Bible answers because they are Phil and Cheryl's kids and not because they are the *preacher's kids*. We want our children to see the many blessings that they enjoy because they are members of a preacher's family, and we try to use as many examples as possible to make these lessons real and tangible.

"*The fruit of the righteous is a tree of life, and he who wins souls is wise,*" Proverbs 11:30. May we learn the lessons of Priscilla and Aquila, develop evangelistic spirits, and be considered fellow workers with our husbands in the kingdom of God.

An Encouraging Word
by Lydia Casey

A s the mother of three young daughters, I've been interested in reading about the way the female mind develops and operates. I learned that the brain of a little girl is different from that of a little boy, even while still inside the womb. It's fascinating to find out what happens with the various hormones present from the very earliest weeks of gestation that will cause boys and girls to act and feel the way they generally do.

As we well know, some scientists theorize that the presence of these hormones and their behavior within the body are merely evolutionary developments. On the other hand, Christians know that everything about the human body is part of a deliberate, brilliant plan by a powerful, all-knowing Creator. David wrote, *"For You formed my inward parts; You covered me in my mother's womb. I will praise You, for I am fearfully and wonderfully made. Marvelous are Your works"* Psalm 139:13–14.

Because of these pronounced differences between men and women's brains, we operate differently and have different needs as we live and work with one another. And because God designed us, we know that we can use these various strengths in our service to Him within the church.

For example, women are more apt to talk things out, to strive for meaningful relationships with one another, and to understand our feelings on a deeper emotional level. We're much more observant of each other's moods and mind sets than many men usually are, and we often enjoy expressing ourselves more than our male counterparts do. As we'll note throughout this chapter, our efforts in this direction can be edifying and productive, but sometimes things can go amiss, and, tragically, much damage to the Lord's work can be done.

One way in which we as women in the church—and, in particular, as the wives of evangelists—can use our innate abilities in the area of communication is by encouraging each other. Christian women are constantly giving each other our time, our special talents or skills, our support, and our love. Ideally, we *freely* give of ourselves, expecting nothing in return, as Matthew 10:8 instructs. Because *"if God so loved us, we also ought to love one another,"* 1 John 4:11. A big part of showing love is offering encouragement to one another.

Back when I worked in radio broadcasting, I met Liz Curtis Higgs, a gifted communicator who had just wrapped up her career in radio and begun a new work project as an "encourager" of women. In the years that have followed our first meeting, Liz has crisscrossed the country speaking before groups of women concerned about doing their best for God and each other. She understands the important role that encouragement plays in the lives of women trying to do what's right. After all, God gives wisdom *liberally* to all who ask for it (James 1:5); should we be any less *liberal* with the love and encouragement we give to each other?

I well remember a particular encounter I had with this remarkable, loving woman. One evening, along with a couple of girlfriends, I attended one of Liz's talks. It had been a long day at work, and I was feeling lonely and disheartened about the recent end of a long-term relationship that I'd hoped would work out better. As I sat listening to Liz speak, I was reminded of the importance of developing inner strength and beauty, and I enjoyed her trademark stories that she tells to help get her points across through laughter.

After I'd had a chance to talk with her briefly, I walked away looking at part of the inscription she'd written in her book I had asked her to sign for me: "To Lydia the beautiful." Believe me, that evening I was feeling anything but beautiful, inside or out. Liz saw that downtrodden, discouraged young woman, and with her thoughtful words, she helped me to get over the hump I was facing in my life. This woman used her God-endowed communication abilities very effectively to reach out and comfort me. She encouraged me.

Let's never forget to look for ways to give encouragement and love to one another. Young mothers are often self-conscious about their parenting success or their children's behavior. A supportive word from an older woman who can find something to admire in that young woman's efforts will go a long way toward making her feel better. Likewise, a young woman can make an older woman's day if she will compliment her on the way she led a class or handled a problem.

If you're a mother with children in Bible classes, tell the teachers how much you appreciate their work with your children. It only takes a moment to thank or praise someone, expressing your sisterly love. Those little notes sent through the mail can be a treasured source of encouragement for years.

I have seen women's faces light up time and again when they are given an unexpected pat on the back. Isn't that a beautiful sight to see? It's so easy to be generous with praise and appreciation if we will just take the time to give them, even if we aren't on the receiving end of as much encouragement as we need or would like to have. In this way, we can be an example to others and perhaps influence them to start being more encouraging of others, too.

Sometimes we might feel frustrated about giving encouragement to others if we're not getting much back in return. It may help at such times to remember that our goal should be to go above and beyond what is required of us, and to do so eagerly and without reservation. In the Sermon on the Mount, Jesus gives clear instructions to those who would follow Him: "*And whoever compels you to go one mile, go with him two,*" Matthew 5:41.

In our efforts to give encouragement and support, it's important to remember that being unreservedly loving is the only way that any gifts can mean anything or truly *profit* anybody,1 Corinthians 13:3. Although at times it's hard, encourage and express your appreciation of your sisters in Christ with a sincere servant's heart, without the expectation of being encouraged and appreciated in return. We must never "...*grow weary while doing good, for in due season we shall reap if we do not lose heart. Therefore, as we have opportunity, let us do good to all, especially to those who are of the household of faith,*" Galatians 6:9–10.

A Word Fitly Spoken

An old Latin proverb says, "It is easier to pull down than to build up." People all over the world and of every era have probably understood the dangers of unjust, destructive criticism and felt its repercussions. When we speak negatively toward and about each other, we are undermining the good things that our speech can accomplish, like encouragement, edification, and teaching.

It seems ironic in light of the evil that is in the world that much of the ongoing battle that diligent Christians wage from day to day is fought internally, against themselves, in defeating the "*evil thoughts of the heart,*" Genesis 6:5. When we're trying to find ways to be more encouraging and less critical of others, how can we hope to help ourselves in the struggle against our own mouths? When we feel under attack by another's criticism of us, how can we avoid feeding the *forest fire* that can be started by that little piece of kindling, the tongue, James 3:5? Sadly, the way we talk to one another can, if we're not careful, be the polar opposite of encouragement.

> *It only takes a moment to thank or praise someone, expressing your sisterly love.*

At times, the wife of the evangelist can be in a unique position within the congregation to do a lot of good. We will regularly be called upon to demonstrate the calm, forgiving spirit that the Scriptures teach, and we will be able to serve as a good example of the right way to handle the tongue if we make the right choices.

An obvious but sometimes overlooked means of avoiding saying something wrong is to stop and think before we speak. One inspired writer tells us to "*be swift to hear, slow to speak, slow to wrath,*" James 1:19. Before we blurt out the latest news about someone, give an opinion about something, or just vent about what's bothering us, we might benefit by asking ourselves some questions. Is this a productive, encouraging thing I'm about to say? Is it going to help the situation, or will it make it worse?

Even if we don't go through the whole process of thinking through these types of questions before going ahead with something we wanted to say, it's possible that the fact that we just stopped to *ask* ourselves those questions will cause us to avoid making a big mistake. Maybe we just need a few minutes sometimes to allow that heated moment to pass, to let tempers cool, to let the topic of conversation be changed, and to be distracted from a difficult subject. This practice of stopping to think before we speak can buy us some valuable time during which we can extinguish the little fire that's starting to burn within and realize that we don't need to say anything, after all.

However, when we do blunder and say something we shouldn't have, is the best tactic to follow the maxim, "Least said, soonest mended?" Perhaps not. If I have created a wrong impression in someone's mind, spoken rashly or angrily, or said something I shouldn't have, is it necessary for me to go to the one or ones who heard me and set the record straight?

Considering the wealth of passages in the Bible dealing with honesty, such as Proverbs 6:16–17 and Colossians 3:9, I believe the sincere Christian's answer to that question is *yes*. I've got to demonstrate humility, apologize, and clear things up. As I mentioned earlier, the evangelist's wife who does this consistently can be an example to those around her and set the proper spiritual tone for the behavior of all the women in the congregation. We need to be ready and willing to say those underused words, "I made a mistake. I'm sorry."

Just imagine what it would be like if the women of an entire congregation were careful in how they spoke to each other, and, if by chance a problem developed, it was cleared up immediately with patient, submissive, and loving attitudes displayed by all! This—and only this—is the atmosphere Christ envisioned for His disciples: "*A new commandment I give to you, that you love one another; as I have loved you, that you also love one another. By this all will know that you are My disciples, if you have love for one another,*" John 13:34–35. Elsewhere we are given the great example of the worthy woman, who "*opens her mouth with wisdom, and on her tongue is the law of kindness,*" Proverbs 31:26. I find the word *law* to be quite instructive in that context; the implication is that being kind at all times is not optional for the child of God.

When I was in college, I was working in the cafeteria alongside another young woman who was also a Christian. One day she overheard me tell several who came through the line a bit of happy news about some mutual friends. After listening to me spread the news two or three times, my cafeteria coworker quietly took that opportunity to caution me about gossiping, reminding me that gossip takes many forms. She chose her words carefully and spoke in a soft and gentle voice.

That was a very long time ago, yet her comments have stuck with me. I am more careful of my speech today because this godly young woman took a moment to correct me. She knew that "*A word fitly spoken is like apples of gold in settings of silver,*" Proverbs 25:11.

What a beautiful, shining picture it is when we women in the church speak to each other encouragingly, kindly, truthfully, and—when necessary—contritely. Tragically, what terrible damage we cause when we do not.

Sometimes it may seem that the wife and children of the preacher are always in the spotlight, continuously enduring the critical scrutiny of congregation members. Unreasonable expectations and unrealistic standards of behavior can be imposed on the evangelist's family. Even if no harm is intended, there can be a sense of pressure being exerted there that can be hard for the family to bear. Some will always encourage us, but there will usually be those who persist in looking at everyone and everything with a critical eye.

Common sense will tell us that no matter what we do or how hard we try we cannot please everybody one hundred percent of the time. We preachers' wives sometimes tend to knock ourselves out teaching classes, taking food to ailing members, visiting the ill in the hospital, cleaning the church building, and writing cards and notes: those are all wonderful endeavors. But we can't be all things to all people, and efforts in that direction can lead to our becoming exhausted, disillusioned, and burned out.

Trying to do everything perfectly can also leave room for being overly sensitive in case something does go wrong. If criticism is expressed, or if disagreements and misunderstandings occur, we have to try our hardest to remain polite and loving. *"Finally, all of you be of one mind, having compassion for one another, love as brothers, be tenderhearted, be courteous; not returning evil for evil or reviling for reviling, but on the contrary, blessing, knowing that you were called to this, that you may inherit a blessing,"* 1 Peter 3:8–9.

When we've done nothing to deserve criticism, we should ignore it if we can. As Christians, we have to be able to tolerate the imperfections and frailties of other people, even when they may hurt us. It helps to remember the apostle Paul's words: *"For do I now persuade men, or God? Or do I seek to please men? For if I still pleased men, I would not be a bondservant of Christ,"* Galatians 1:10. If we know we're doing everything we can do to please God, unfair treatment by others won't sting nearly as much.

Further, if I have been unjustly criticized and might have every right to be upset, I must not retaliate in anger. Even if, from a worldly perspective, my rebuttal is crying out to be heard, I would be wise to take a moment to recall these commands:

> *Repay no one evil for evil. . . . If it is possible, as much as depends on you, live peaceably with all men. Beloved, do not avenge yourselves, but rather give place to wrath; for it is written, 'Vengeance is Mine, I will repay,' says the Lord. Therefore if your enemy is hungry, feed him; If he is thirsty, give him a drink; For in so doing you will heap coals of fire on his head. Do not be overcome by evil, but overcome evil with good,* Romans 12:17–21.

Greater Love Has No One Than This

Do you know everyone in your congregation equally well? Are there some people whom you talk to all the time, while there are others who slip in and out of the church building unnoticed? When there are visitors during your worship services, do you dash over to shake their hands and make their acquaintance, while members who might really like to talk with you lose their opportunity to spend some time together? How can we encourage each other as we ought to, if we hardly know each other?

The importance of forging strong relationships with fellow Christians is stressed by the apostle Peter: *"Since you have purified your souls in obeying the truth through the Spirit in sincere love of the brethren, love one another fervently with a pure heart,"* 1 Peter 1:22.

By cultivating loving friendships with as many as we possibly can within our congregations, we will be in a better position to extend encouragement when the need arises. The spiritual and emotional support we need to offer our sisters and brothers from time to time will mean more and be much more effective if we have strong relationships with them already in place.

My oldest daughter and I recently went on a field trip to New York City where we saw Ground Zero, complete with cranes and bulldozers. Viewing the remains of what used to stand at that location called to mind a TV documentary I saw a few years ago concerning the destruction of the World Trade Center. I had been riveted by the story of three office friends who were trying to make it out of one of the towers. As they stumbled down the smoky stairwell, with firemen ascending the stairs next to them, they were surely aware of the dire need to get out as quickly as they could. Yet one of the men was having a lot of trouble continuing, and he had to stop to rest several times. His two companions pleaded with him to get up and keep going. He refused, saying he just couldn't make it.

After still more urging, and with obvious reluctance, one of the men resumed his flight down the stairs to safety on his own. The other man stayed with his exhausted friend, continuing to beg him to get on his feet. After a while, he was able to start moving slowly down the stairs again, leaning heavily on the man who had stayed behind with him, say witnesses who passed by on their own way down. Tragically, the two did not make it out of the tower before it collapsed, and they lost their lives.

Jesus said, *"This is my commandment, that you love one another as I have loved you. Greater love has no one than this, than to lay down one's life for his friends,"* John 15:12–13. If we aspire to the *great love* that

Christ was instructing His apostles to have for each other, with laying down one's life as the ultimate expression of that love, we must be willing to demonstrate other attributes of true friendship as well.

One way to make sure our friendships within our congregations grow to be as strong as they should is to treat each other well, being careful of each other's feelings. There are many things we can do to promote a friendly, encouraging mood among the Christians with whom we worship.

For example, by our choices in our associations, do we contribute to the development of cliques within our congregations? Can we think back to our high school days when we might have been ostracized from a group we wanted to fit in with? A good rule of thumb to follow in talking about social events is that if everybody isn't invited, don't talk about it in front of everybody! We need to do whatever we can to discourage cliques from existing within a congregation, as they most definitely do not lead to a spiritually strong, united atmosphere.

Kindness and thoughtfulness in our actions should be second nature to us as Christian women, but sometimes they aren't—perhaps not out of a deliberate desire to wound another person, but because we just don't stop and think about what the other person might be thinking or feeling. We must *resolve* to be kind and thoughtful toward each other, not only do it when it's convenient or when we just happen to think of it as we rush through our days.

Congregations of the Lord's people can be joyful bands of committed Christians who, as true friends, genuinely love each other. Unfortunately, a congregation can also be a collection of strangers who barely speak to each other before and after each worship service and never see each other outside of the meeting place. Members of some congregations divide themselves into exclusive social groups and rarely circulate outside them. In these cases, little is accomplished, it would seem, toward the collective goal of winning souls to Christ. These behaviors do not fit into the picture of love, mutual encouragement, and true friendship that Christ wants for His people.

However, even the best of friendships can hit a rocky patch. When we slip up and hurt each other, either by design or by neglect, our response to the situation says a lot about how seriously we take our responsibilities as Christians. If I have caused a problem, I need to fix it as quickly and painlessly as possible. My jobs are to say that I was wrong and that I am sorry, and to make sure that everyone has come to a peaceful understanding of what happened. To do less is to invite a buildup of resentment in the heart of the person I hurt, and that certainly

> *Kindness and thoughtfulness in our actions should be second nature to us as Christian women.*

will not promote a positive, encouraging environment within the congregation.

But what if I am the one who has been mistreated or hurt? What are my responsibilities as a Christian in that case? First, I should control my irritation and not spread the news of my injured feelings around to anyone who'll listen. Even if I have not been asked to, I must compassionately forgive the person who hurt me and not harbor a grudge against her, as Matthew 18:21–22 and Luke 6:37 clearly teach.

I suppose that one of the many things we all enjoy so much about babies is that they don't hold grudges. I remember watching one of my daughters scare her little sister out of her wits with a loud noise or a sudden movement, and the next minute the baby would be all smiles and giggles again. The baby quickly forgot the unpleasantness of the past, focusing on the thrill of the moment. She didn't hold her older sister's mistakes over her head indefinitely or until some punishment had been enforced. Babies know how to move on.

Couldn't we adults be more like that? Couldn't we bounce back quickly from the annoying things that happen and get on with the important things in life, like loving and encouraging each other? The apostle Paul warns against hanging onto things like *bitterness* and *malice* and urges us instead to *"be kind to one another, tenderhearted, forgiving one another, even as God in Christ forgave you,"* Ephesians 4:31–32.

When something goes wrong and threatens to thwart new progress toward our goals as Christians, it may help to remember Paul's encouraging words to the Philippians concerning their faith: *"forgetting those things which are behind and reaching forward to those things which are ahead, I press toward the goal for the prize of the upward call of God in Christ Jesus,"* Philippians 3:13–14.

The vital importance of forgiveness in our lives cannot be understated. We must never stop being hopeful for spiritual growth both in ourselves and in others. We must never stop encouraging each other to be the best we can possibly be in every way that is pleasing to God. We must never fall victim to cynicism, thinking that others can't change for the better. Paul instructed the Christians in Thessalonica to *"be patient with all,"* 1 Thessalonians 5:14.

We ourselves need some compassionate understanding and forgiveness at times, and we must always be willing to extend that same patient sympathy to those around us when they struggle. In this way, we can be a desperately needed source of encouragement to others. God's word allows very little space in the Christian's heart for cynicism, suspicion, and skepticism about our sisters and brothers in Christ. If we hope to have real, loving friendships upon which the most complete spiritual relationships can be built, we can't afford to give up on each other.

Yes, boys and girls are formed differently in the womb, and their brains develop differently. From infancy, they grow up to be men and women whose lives, behavior, and words evidence these differences that our Creator designed.

We can misuse our physiological uniqueness as women to send us down wrong paths marked by behaviors like gossiping, backstabbing, or being ruled by our emotions. We can allow ourselves to be manipulative, jealous, or overly competitive, and we can become too critical of others and hypersensitive to criticism ourselves.

On the other hand, we can use our feminine gifts of intuitiveness, boundless compassion, nurturing ability, and communicativeness to serve the Lord and His church. We can love deeply, from the bottom of our hearts, and we can cultivate true friendships with our sisters and brothers in Christ. We can *"consider one another in order to stir up love and good works,"* helping each other be productive citizens of the kingdom and make it to heaven, Hebrews 10:24.

And, dear sisters, as we travel this road together, we can take every opportunity to reach out and encourage each other all along the way.

Alone Among Many
—*Who will Build Me Up?*—
by Dana Burk

Glass Houses

You know how you hear things and you believe them . . . well . . . sorta. Anyway, I had heard about her bathroom, but hadn't seen it. We were among the few invited that evening to visit after a gospel meeting and as we arrived someone whispered, "You have to see the powder room. Totally mirrors." I nodded, greeted the hosts and began to mingle with friends and new acquaintances. After refreshments and coffee I excused myself to use this novelty of a *powder room*. It **was** totally mirrored. The walls, the ceiling, the floor, even the fixtures were mirrored or bright shining chrome. I stood in the center of the room in awe just slowly turning as I gazed at every angle that seemed to go on forever. I had never seen anything quite like it. Nothing was hidden. . . . **Oh! Nothing was hidden!!!** I began to realize as I situated myself to take care of personal business that there was no privacy in that bathroom, not even from me. I'm not sure why exactly, but I was quite uncomfortable, feeling . . . well, totally exposed, even though I was the only one in the room. Admittedly, the room was spectacular, but I decided I wouldn't want a totally mirrored powder room in my dream house (not that we were about to stumble across the money to build one anyway); definitely, too much exposure.

The feeling I had in that bathroom that night is how I often feel as a *preacher's wife*. Too much exposure! Nothing is hidden in the glass houses we dwell in. All is laid wide open for everyone to see. We are never those families who come in late, sit on the back row, and because we leave first, no one knows us. No, not only do they know us, but they know everything about us . . . or do they? Because we are so *popular*, so *in the limelight*, we are constantly surrounded by friends. . . . Really? In fact, we are so deeply loved by our congregational family that we can turn to any one of them with our problems. . . . Better **not!**

The seemingly open book of a preacher's life and the life of his wife and family can be very deceiving. The life of a preacher and subsequently of his wife can be a lonely one. And I think, because of the very nature of women, the natural desire of women to have a best friend, to have a girlfriend to confide in, shop with, and just talk to, a preacher's wife's life can be at times, painfully lonely. She will often find herself *alone among many*. She may be surrounded by 40, 50, 100, or even 300 loving members of a congregation, but due to the ever present concern of, *what will people think* or *what will people say*, she withdraws into a quiet world alone. I have found myself there often.

There are few members of the congregations my husband has preached for that I have allowed myself to fully confide in. When we were much younger, naively I trusted sisters only to feel betrayed when my husband would preach on a subject some members of the congregation wanted banned. It was amazing how things you had said in confidence could be twisted and misconstrued. It always seemed that the sisters, who had been the first to help you, love you, and make you feel welcome when you moved to a new congregation were the first to betray your confidence. My lack of trust became so intense that I found I had built a wall, a shield around myself and made certain no one penetrated it. As I have gotten older, I have become wiser at choosing my friends.

My Friends

We all need a friend, a best friend. Someone we can trust with our deepest secrets and most painful hurts. Someone who truly understands . . . **me**. We need to allow someone to penetrate through that wall, that shield that we subconsciously erect and allow them to be a support to us because we all need one; a support to help get through the rough times, the lonely times each of us will face. We all need someone to build us up while life's trials are tearing us down. Here are mine. I have three:

my LORD, my husband, and my daughter—in that order. Let me tell you about them in reverse.

My Daughter . . .

GOD blessed me with a daughter, my first child. She is a beautiful young woman who loves GOD and serves Him faithfully and she probably understands me better than any other woman alive. (My mother has been dead for over 20 years or she would be at the top of the list.) My daughter and I share a great deal: our accomplishments, our frustrations, our sorrows, our joys and even our weaknesses. I tell her when she is doing great and I never fail to tell her when she isn't. I must confess, she tells me the same things. My life would be quite empty without her. But . . . she is my daughter and there are those things that, as a mother, I do not feel I should burden her with, and I don't.

A preacher's wife's life can be at times, painfully lonely.

(You might not have the daughter I have, who in her adult life has become my girlfriend, shopping friend, confidant, support, etc. Maybe yours is your mother, a sister in the flesh or even a sister in the church you have grown close to over the years. I hope you have a woman you love as a friend, trust completely and are close to—you need that. She will understand you like no man ever can.)

My Husband . . .

I have an incredible husband. Tol is kind, generous, and above all else he is the most selfless person I know—and I do not exaggerate. He will do basically anything for me (and for that matter, anyone else). I am spoiled. Anyone who knows us very well at all will agree . . . I am **spoiled**! There is only one thing that he is more passionate about than me and that is the *mission* work that he does throughout the Caribbean and South America. We have been friends for decades and been through a great deal together. We have raised three children together and are now blessed with five grandchildren. We have buried two parents together; his father, my mother. We have moved repeatedly together. We have moved to numerous states, lived overseas for a third of our married life, and worked in various cultures together. We have built homes together and lost homes to a hurricane and fire together. We have lived life side by side and are bonded as only a married couple can be. I understand him like no other and he knows me the same. We know each other's thoughts and finish each other's sentences. We know when we need to comfort one another and we know when each other needs their space. We are best friends! But . . . he is my husband which means he is a man . . . and there are things he just doesn't understand.

I said earlier that there is only one thing that my husband is more passionate about than me and that is the work he does for the Lord, the mission work he does throughout the Caribbean and South America. I suspect most dedicated preachers of the Lord's gospel are much like my guy. Tol has no hobbies, watches no TV, and watches no sports to speak of, except the occasional football game that I shame him into watching with me. (I am the sports fan in the family.) He has no buddies he hangs out with. . . . Tol just works. He is a workaholic in the true sense of the word. He spends countless hours studying, writing, and corresponding with Christians literally all over the world . . . always teaching, always encouraging others—remember, I told you he was the most selfless person I know. Tol's office is in our home, the room next to our bedroom, and yet it feels like there are days we see very little of each other except at meal time and bed time.

Tol also travels—he travels a lot. He is gone somewhere nearly every month and sometimes for two weeks at a time. When he is gone, we often have little communication because of the lack of telephone signals or lack of computer access available in the many remote places he travels to. My husband is my best friend ... when he is around. And, at the moment, we live in the foreign culture of Puerto Rico, in a city of 2½ million people who speak Spanish, a language I do not speak and I often feel *alone among many*. My husband is fluent in Spanish and though he says he understands my loneliness, he doesn't ... he can't.

Don't misunderstand me—I wouldn't trade my guy for any other on the planet. He tries to comfort me, care for me, provide for me and support me to the best of his ability. He is, without a doubt, the only one who would *put up* with me and, as I frequently remind him, I am the only one who would *put up* with him. My life wouldn't be my life if it were not for Tol—and I have a good life. I guess, in a way, we define together who we really are individually. I love him and thank my gracious GOD for him. But ... my husband and I are still separate individuals who do not go through the same experiences or share the same emotions due simply to the fact that he is male and I am female. If you are married, you are in the same situation. You may have an awesome husband, but he still can't understand all that sorrow, fear, loss, passion, love, loneliness, anger, pain, concern, shock, embarrassment, elation, etc., etc.—that incredible depth and range of emotions that you go through within the first thirty minutes of your getting out of bed each morning, not to mention the rest of the emotions you encounter throughout your day. He is a man, and literally thank GOD, he just doesn't go through all that emotional stuff we do (it's a good thing someone in the family can keep their emotions intact), so ... how can he totally understand?

My LORD ...

But I do have a best friend that does understand, and understands everything. I do have a best friend with whom I can share everything. You know where I'm going with this —it is my LORD. And He and I talk often.

Paul poses the question in 1 Corinthians 2:11, *"For what man knows the things of a man except the spirit of the man which is in him?"*

He rhetorically affirms the only man who knows and understands the very deepest thoughts and feelings of a man is the man himself (or woman as the case may be). That's the point I've been trying to make. Yet we are told there is One who knows us...truly **knows** us.

> *O* Lord, *You have searched me and known me.*
> *You know my sitting down and my rising up;*
> *You understand my thought afar off.*
> *You comprehend my path and my lying down,*
> *And are acquainted with all my ways.*
> *For there is not a word on my tongue,*
> *But behold, O LORD, You know it altogether,* Psalm 139:1–4.

So, it is only the LORD that can truly know me and understand me . . . all there is to know and understand about me down into my very soul. And most remarkably, though He knows all about me: all my fabulous personality characteristics, all my incredible and unique talents, all my generous good works and unlimited kindness . . . all my resentment, all my selfishness, all my anger, my hatred, my pride—He still loves me.

The LORD is my friend . . . **my very best friend!** He does not pump me up by stroking my ego nor disown me because of my faults and weaknesses. He just simply loves ME. He is such a friend that I feel no shame when I cry in His presence—He never says I'm too emotional. I have no worry of Him betraying my confidence—I can tell Him anything. He does not judge me because of my beauty or lack thereof, my size, my economic means, education, race (He created me), or citizenship. He understands the deep, crushing hurt and pain I still feel twenty years after the death of my mother and doesn't tell me I should be over it by now—He just understands. He knows I really am sweating and hot even when the thermostat says it is 64 and He also knows I really do **have to have** that chocolate bar **now**! He doesn't ridicule me when I wake Him after hearing the third bump in the night following that late, late mystery movie—He just tells me He will stay up and watch through the night for me. He understands why I lay awake all night waiting to hear my child arrived safely—He watched for and saw His son while he was still a great way off. He knows how severe the pain is from my physical condition—I've never heard Him say I was a wimp. He understands the depression I suffer from due to my chronic illness or constant loneliness or the financial condition I have got myself into again . . . and He promises to never leave me nor forsake me. In fact, He reminds me that all of this is temporary and it will be OK one day—He will take care of everything. And I know He **can** take care of everything—He is my GOD, my SAVIOR, my REDEEMER, my KING, my FRIEND—MY VERY BEST FRIEND!

It is with the help of my best friend, the LORD, that I get through the trials of being a preacher's wife, that I am able to live in that *glass house* and with His help that I just get through life. When I am on the verge of *burn out* after my feeble efforts of trying to teach, encourage, and lift others up, He is always there to lift me up . . . no, to hold me up and lead me through anything that life brings my way. What does that poem say . . . it was then "when I carried you." And so, you see, I am never completely alone.

My Friend's Plan

OK, we all know the LORD is our best friend and is there to help us with all our needs. We know He gave us His word to instruct us and encourage us through our daily walk with Him. We also know that what He says is always best, even when we don't see it or understand it . . . and sometimes when we don't even believe it. So, how do we use what we know? What is our Very Best Friend's plan, our LORD'S plan for support, comfort, and friendship?

Find a Friend . . .

The proverb tells us, *"As iron sharpens iron, so a man sharpens the countenance of his friend,"* Proverbs 27:17. The wise man says in

Ecclesiastes 4:9–12:

> *Two are better than one,*
> *Because they have a good reward for their labor.*
> *For if they fall, one will lift up his companion.*
> *But woe to him who is alone when he falls,*
> *For he has no one to help him up.*
> *Again, if two lie down together, they will keep warm;*
> *But how can one be warm alone?*
> *Though one may be overpowered by another, two can*
>   *withstand him.*
> *And a threefold cord is not quickly broken.*

It is always easier to get through a difficult situation if you have someone beside you. In fact, our lives revolve and are completely built around relationships with others. Even the introvert has no desire to go through life totally **alone**. It is noteworthy that Christ Himself sought out friends in His last hours. He called His closest disciples to go with Him and watch for Him while He prayed that last night here on earth. He spent hours talking with His FATHER. And, at that last moment,

> *He is such a friend that I feel no shame when I cry in His presence.*

He cried out in deep despair, *"My God, My God, why have You forsaken Me?"* Matthew 27:46. Man was designed for relationships. Wasn't it God Himself who said, *"It is not good that man should be alone."?* We need a friend. We need to find someone we can trust, we can love, and we can confide in. Hopefully you have that kind of friend in your husband or a family member, but what about when they aren't around . . . when they can't be around? You still need a friend.

Find the Right Kind of Friend . . .

We all know evil companions corrupt good morals and I trust none of us are seeking out worldly, evil friendships . . . however, just because someone is a *good* person doesn't mean she is a *godly* person. Just because someone likes to shop at the same boutique you do, or wears the same make-up as you, just because she takes her kids to the same park as you or your kids are on the same ball team, just because you go to the same work-out class or bump into each other every day at the track, just because you play bridge together or are on the same bowling league, just because you both like tennis, scrabble, fine art, Starbuck's white mocha lattes and lemon crumb cake does not mean you have things in common—at least it doesn't mean you have what is important in common. It doesn't mean she should be your best friend if she isn't a Christian.

In Second Corinthians six, Paul encourages the brethren at Corinth to separate themselves from ungodly relationships in this world and not be *unequally yoked* to them. He states,

> *Do not be unequally yoked together with unbelievers. For*
> *what fellowship has righteousness with lawlessness? And*
> *what communion has light with darkness? And what ac-*
> *cord has Christ with Belial? Or what part has a believer*
> *with an unbeliever? And what agreement has the temple*
> *of God with idols? For you are the temple of the living*
> *God. As God has said:*
> *'I will dwell in them*
> *And walk among them.*
> *I will be their God,*
> *And they shall be My people."*
> *Therefore,*
> *"Come out from among them*
> *And be separate, says the Lord.*
> *Do not touch what is unclean,*
> *And I will receive you."*

"I will be a Father to you,
And you shall be My sons and daughters,
Says the LORD Almighty," 2 Corinthians 6:14–18.

This is not to say that we cannot have casual friendships with people in the world . . . we will still walk the track with them, exercise beside them, shop at the same boutique and I plan to keep on drinking Starbuck's mocha lattes and eating lemon crumb cake, but that doesn't mean I will depend on worldly friends as my support when I am struggling and lonely, when I am weak spiritually, when I need someone to confide in. How could a casual friend from the world know how to best comfort me with the promises of God when I am sad, know how to correct me when I am wrong, know how to encourage me to follow God when I am weak, or know where to tell me to take my burdens when they are too heavy for me to carry? A friend without God cannot point me to God.

Jesus had friends in the world. In fact, He was accused of being *"a friend of tax collectors and sinners,"* Luke 7:34. But it was not these friends He turned to in His times of need. He turned to those who shared His spiritual goals and ideals. I owned a small dog boutique and grooming salon a few years ago and had several employees who worked for me. A young lady moved to our area who was a new Christian, who had no spiritual support at home and no godly friends in the area. I hired her to work for me—not because I needed her (I didn't), but because she needed me. I told her that several months later as we were discussing the need for choosing godly friends. Jesus often sought out friends in the world, not because He *needed* them, but because *they* needed Him. When He needed comfort and support to face the trials ahead of Him, He chose godly men to surround Himself with and GOD to confide in and lean on. And He is our example in all things . . . especially in choosing friends. Sometimes, God gives us friends, not because they need us, but because we need them.

Find a Christian Friend . . .

I am a very private person. There are few people in this world that *really* know **me**. I am extremely modest and by that I mean I do not like to share bathrooms, showers, locker rooms or anything of the sort even with other women. I'd really rather not even share a hotel room with anyone other than my husband and that even includes my own family. I like my own private space. When I come out of my room for the day to face the world, I want my hair done, clothes matching, make-up on and earrings in . . . that is the way I want people to know me. Pride—I know. But I suppose it is also that *glass house* I have lived in most of my life, that *preacher's wife* syndrome that so many of us face everyday—the feeling that I must be perfect (or at least as perfect as I can appear) lest anyone find fault with me and judge me. Maybe it isn't pride but rather insecurity. (That's a scary thought.) I don't like thinking of myself as insecure anymore than I like thinking of myself as proud, but I guess it is true to some extent. So you can imagine how difficult I find it to divulge my weaknesses, my imperfections, dare I say my sins to someone else. They might find out who I *really* am. I suspect I am not that much different from you. I suspect you may suffer from some of the same privacy issues and insecurities that I do. Do we then really **need** to have a best friend here on earth? Yeah, we do.

I tried for a long time to make it through this life without close, close friends. I am independent, a self-starter, and besides, I have the LORD to help me when I need a friend. I didn't realize for many years that my Mom was my close, close friend . . . at least I didn't realize it until she was gone. Then for a number of years I struggled on with life living off in the Caribbean, alone with my husband and family and things got a little tougher. Things got a little lonelier. But it was OK because I had my husband around and when he wasn't, when he traveled, I still had my children around to keep me busy. Then they grew up, moved away, and there I was . . . "alone again, naturally." Remember that song? Ever feel that way?

I don't think I realized how vitally important close Christian friends really were until we lost our home to a fire just a few months after moving to Tennessee. That was the beginning of some very dear friendships for me . . . some I know will never end and some I know helped me make it through some extremely lonely, frustrating, and sorrowful times. And I still depend on those friendships today. When you lose everything, and I do mean everything except the clothes you are wearing, you find out who your real friends are. They do not love you because of what you have—you have nothing . . . how you dress—you are only wearing hand-me-downs they gave you . . . or how *together* you are—because you aren't. They love you . . . the real you, the insecure, needy you, just because you are you and that's a humbling feeling, yet a very refreshing one. Your glass house is shattered and they see right through you. They see your tears, your anger, your inadequacy, your frustrations and they still love you. And these kinds of friends help you put your life back together, without judging you and help you keep it going. I found out during a very dark time in my life that I needed those kinds of friends. And the LORD placed me smack dab in the middle of a whole congregation of those kinds of friends. He showed me I needed them much more than they ever needed me.

Shortly after that and repeatedly for the next several years I found out I continued to need them. I have severe asthma, a husband who travels, and three kids spread out over three states other than the one I live in. Invariably, I will have a severe bout with my asthma and end up in the hospital when Tol is out of the country. It's not like the kids can just pop in the car and be across town to help me...I have had to depend on those really close friends. I have had to expose myself, swallow my pride, tear down my walls and ask for help.

I remember the first time I **had** to have help. I had spent the entire night at home alone, too proud or stubborn to call someone to come sit with me, with each breath wondering if I would be able to take my next one, just waiting for the clock to ring 8:00 AM so I could call my doctor. I foolishly drove myself across town to his office, staggered in, turned around and drove myself to the hospital where my doctor had already called ahead and pre-admitted me. On the way, I knew I **had** to have some help. I had a dog at home alone, no clothes, no toiletries, and no one knowing I was sick, and worst of all, I didn't have the breath to call and talk. I had missed ladies Bible class that morning. In fact, my doctor's office was just a few blocks past the church building and I had seen the sisters' cars gathered in the parking lot on my way to the hospital. All I would have to have done was stop, and anyone of them would have come with me immediately . . . but, no—too proud. As I approached the hospital I flipped mentally through the list of ladies at church I would feel most comfortable about calling to help me. I checked off a number of them because of their work schedules, family obligations, own health concerns, the proximity of where they lived to where I was and finally decided to call Jauhyn. She was about my age, had three grown children like me and a husband who traveled a lot, like mine—she would understand and not judge that aspect of my situation. She arrived only moments after I got into my room, scolding me for having waited so long to ask for help. I gave her my keys, instructions where things were, and the name of the dog kennel.

> *We have each other we can confide in if no one else.*

One of the most private things about me is my laundry (silly, I know) . . . I'll let you do a lot for me, but please, please, leave my clothes alone. I'll take care of them myself. And don't go prowling in my dresser drawers and personal life. Well, Jauhyn prowled through my drawers, rummaged through my clothes, and did my laundry for a week. She ended up taking my little yorkie, Layla, home with her and has become, to this day, my dearest Christian friend outside of my family. I know she loves ME, not because I have it all together, always look my best, or because I can do for her. She just loves me as a friend and I have often needed her. She has helped me get through some very tough times in my life when no one else was there. We have shared many private things over the years as sisters in Christ. We have laughed together, cried together, gone to ladies weekends together, fretted about the church together, and prayed together. We live thousands of miles apart today, but I still cherish the brief moments I can spend with her from time to time. My yorkie, Layla, still gets excited if you talk about *Auntie Jauhyn* and this friend is always welcome to prowl through my dresser drawers. Because of this friend, I have learned to open myself up to other friends and my life is richer, fuller, and much less lonely because I let other Christians into my life.

It was our Very Best Friend, the LORD, who set up the church, the perfect support group, to help each of us make it through the trials and struggles of this life. Ephesians four tells us that He established those in the church to instruct us and guide us for the purpose of edifying the body, for the building up of the church and in verse sixteen the writer tells us that each part (person) must do its share, causing growth in the body of Christ through love. The Apostle Paul tells us in Galatians 6:2 to *"Bear one another's burdens."* The very way that is stated indicates that not only should I be willing to help my sister in Christ with her burdens, but I must be willing to allow her to help me with mine. The LORD knows what we need, even when we don't believe it ourselves.

I had someone say to me one time, "When you refuse to accept or ask for help from your brother or sister in Christ, you are robbing them of blessings from their Heavenly Father." So often we refuse to open ourselves up to the friendship and help of others because we are protecting (often falsely) ourselves from the potential of hurt, but we are also stealing the blessings of friendship from them as well. *"Bear one another's burdens, and so fulfill the Law of Christ,"* Galatians 6:2. They have the right to reap rewards of their good works as much as I do. I need to let them in and let them love me, not only for my benefit, but for theirs as well.

Risks of Friendship

Do you remember the words of that song Bette Midler sang back in '79, titled "The Rose"? The first two stanzas read:

Some say love, it is a river
That drowns the tender reed
Some say love, it is a razor
That leaves your soul to bleed
Some say love, it is a hunger,
An endless aching need
I say love, it is a flower,
And you, its only seed
It's the heart, afraid of breaking
That never learns to dance
It's the dream, afraid of waking
That never takes the chance
It's the one who won't be taken
Who cannot seem to give
And the soul, afraid of dying
That never learns to live

Friendship is risky business. Exposing your fragile ego and laying it wide open to possibly be trampled upon, criticized, ridiculed, and falsely judged is scary business. Sometimes we are so afraid of being hurt that we never learn how to love, laugh, or live. We stay so deeply withdrawn in our own little world making certain no one can reach our fragile inside, no one can touch the delicate parts of our soul that we never know the depths of love and joy that can only come through deep, caring, meaningful relationships with other people. We forget that it is these relationships, and only these relationships that have any real and lasting meaning in life anyway. "*Naked I came from my mother's womb, and naked shall I return there,*" Job 1:21. The only thing I will take with me someday, the only thing that will have eternal consequences in my life is the love that I have developed through relationships with others. What will I take with me if I have none?

Jesus felt it worth the risk of exposing himself to rejection. He developed many friendships and, as we all know too well, lost His life because of one in particular. He allowed His betrayer to become an extremely close friend, intimate, personal. He was rejected by His own family, His best friends, His countrymen, His disciples. Yet He counted it worth the cost. He knew the rewards far outweighed the risks and pain of rejection. If He had not allowed mankind to come to know Him so well, so personally, so intimately, you and I would not know how much He loved us and He would never have invited us into His eternal life. He had to open Himself up to the very real possibility that I would reject Him in order for Him to save me and ask me to spend eternity with Him. I'm so glad He was willing to suffer rejection in order to find true friendship.

Preacher's Wife to Preacher's Wife/Elder's Wife

As preachers' and as elders' wives, we often get on our soap boxes about how we are no different from all the other members of the church and how we should not have to live according to a double standard, etc., etc. But that is just a soap box, not reality. We do live according to a double standard, always have and always will. Standing on top of that box ranting and raving, protesting and whining will not remove the glass walls but will only impede the work we have to do. We just need to step down out of the clouds, roll up our sleeves and keep working the best we know how, realizing there will always be those who never think we are good enough. That's OK. Thank God, they won't be judging me where it really counts. He will be.

We also need to remember there are hundreds, I suppose even thousands of sisters across this globe who are in our exact shoes. They are a preacher's wife or an elder's wife being judged by that same double standard. Though I often feel alone among many, I am not alone in this.

Remember when God told Elisha, *"Yet I have reserved seven thousand in Israel, all whose knees have not bowed to Baal, and every mouth that has not kissed him,"* 1 Kings 19:18. Elisha was feeling very alone, very sorry for himself. God wanted him to know that he was not alone and neither are you, my sister. I, Dana Burk, am right there with you. So are Joyce and Joanne, Becky and Lydia, Cindy, Dena, Cheryl and Julie. Along with all the Mary's and Cathy's, Sarah's and Rachel's, Kelly's and Kim's, Joan's and Alice's, Patricia's, Virginia's, Christy's and [*you fill in your name*] who stand beside their husbands in the work as servants of God.

We have each other we can confide in if no one else. We as preachers' and elders' wives should be able to connect with other sisters who will truly understand our burdens when we feel we can turn to no one else. After all, I can understand what you are going through. I doubt that there is much, if anything, you can tell me I haven't already heard or experienced myself. Having trouble raising a teenager . . . I raised three. Lost a parent . . . so have I. Financial troubles . . . I'm wondering when mine will cease. Reputation tainted by gossip . . . could I tell you some tales. Struggling with your temper . . . I fight with mine daily. Unfaithful husband . . . I haven't, but some of my dearest friends have had one. A husband caught up in pornography . . . not mine, but a friend who was like my own son. Family member with drug problems, gambling problems, sexual problems, jealousy, etc., etc. . . . If I haven't been through these personally, someone I know has and so has someone most preacher's and elder's wives know. You see, we are all very much alike. We all deal with personal demons and struggles and the demons and struggles of our families and friends. We can help one another when we need a friend. Just because we may not worship in the same congregation, live in the same town, or for that matter the same country, we have each other we can lean on as a support, someone who can help us get through life.

My grandmother used to say, "They can call them the 'good ole days' and I guess they were, but I don't want to go back to them." Good point. You know, we live in one of the best of times in my opinion. We can be in New York this morning and home in bed in LA tonight. I live, at this moment, in the Caribbean, but can pick up my cell phone, call my kids in Kentucky, Georgia, or Florida and sound like we are next door. Even more remarkably, my husband can call me on Skype from South America, turn on his webcam and we talk to each other face to face as though he were in the next room. E-mail, now Facebook and Twitter have us all connected at record speeds. Granted, we can connect to spread gossip faster than ever before which, of course, is still as wrong as ever before, but we can also connect to strengthen and support one another in a way the church has never seen until now. We need to utilize the avenues and connections God has given us to befriend one another as we each make our way back home to Him. Find another preacher's wife or elder's wife you can share you pains, struggles, fears, joys, triumphs, and frustrations with. You will be richer for it and so will those whom you serve as you stay refreshed and strong for them because of the love and strength you draw from your new friend.

Our LORD'S plan is that we never be alone. He wants us to make connections and build relationships with others. He wants us to have strong family ties, healthy marriages and relationships with our spouses, but He also knows we need friendships with like-minded brothers and sisters whose goals and desires, struggles and frustrations are the same as our own. And, above all, He wants us to remember . . . *"He Himself has said, 'I will never leave you nor forsake you,'"* Hebrews 13:5.

It Comes with the Territory
by Joyce Jamerson

I f you are a sportsman, you can expect injuries; a cook is likely to get burned; the doctor will surely be interrupted by phone calls at almost any hour and preachers—yes, there are occupational hazards there too. It comes with the territory. This expression has been around for a long time; made popular by Willy, a character in Arthur Miller's book, *The Death of a Salesman*.

Every line of work has positives and negatives. We accept that there will be difficulties along the road of life and deal with the negatives as they happen, but at the same time are encouraged by the positives. If it were not for so many positives, the road traveled would be long and dreary, but there are many who depend on the spiritual leadership provided by the preacher and his wife. Preachers and their families can be challenged day by day, never quite knowing what is coming next! And when we think we've experienced it all, here comes something new. (Sin is inventive, isn't it?) Each place provides a new dynamic and a new challenge. Some places are ready for a new and exciting outlook. Some are sluggish and need a boost, and at some you may have to find a way to break the code. You are an outsider and always will be an outsider. They had their own way of doing things before you got there, and will continue on when you leave.

Negativity can become a way of life, and we have to learn to combat that with positive thinking. It would be easy to get caught up in negativity of others, but we need to promote a positive outlook as much as possible. One of the most difficult things for a preacher's wife to do is to stay silent when her husband is being criticized. It's natural to want to come to his defense, but doing so will give the impression that he is weak. We can heartily come to his defense in the privacy of our homes. Even harder is to have your children unjustly criticized especially when there is a double standard for them as opposed to children of other members.

At times, no comment at all is best. A long time ago two of the children and I had been out of town visiting my parents, returning just in time for Sunday evening services. This was before cell phones and Frank was a little concerned about my arrival. When I entered the lobby, he met me there and gave me a quick kiss. One of the good sisters thought such a public display of affection was out of place and didn't hesitate to let others around her know how she felt. We totally ignored her little tantrum. *It comes with the territory.*

A sense of humor is vital because you just have to laugh when you're repeatedly called the name of the previous preacher's wife, or told that your biscuits aren't as good as the ones she made! Women have a reputation for being catty, but they aren't the only ones who can make unkind comments. During a gospel meeting, the visiting preacher had on a sport coat with a rather prominent design. One of the elders spoke to him and told him, "I'm sorry your horse died," insinuating that his sport coat would have made a suitable blanket. The preacher was so taken back with that comment, he had little to say. We knew it was probably meant as a joke but some jokes are just out of place. The ability to politely field thoughtless comments comes with practice. It's aggravating to accompany your husband to a gospel meeting, going to one—perhaps two services a day, and come home to be asked, *how was your vacation?* Some meetings are jam packed with visiting, classes, and meals and there's little time for anything else. It may have been a very pleasant time or it may have been fraught with problem solving and difficulty. We return home either uplifted or exhausted and having a different definition of vacation!

There was a period of time when working outside the home was a necessity because our boys were quickly reaching college age and we had not been able to save for their education on our current salary. Trying to balance work, the duties of home, and four children plus church work can stretch even the best of planners. When going to a potluck planned for a visiting preacher, Frank had to go pick up some item that had been forgotten in the rush and as I was arranging some items on the table, a sister was heard to say to another, "Our poor little preacher, he has to do everything himself." The retorts that went through my mind thankfully were never spoken! *It comes with the territory.*

When conducting the poll mentioned in the introduction and chapter one, those participating were asked to finish the following sentence. The answers are very revealing and give some insight to problems that can be faced.

Brethren have no right to:

♦ Hold the preacher's wife to a different standard from the one applying to all Christians.

♦ Expect the same thing from me as from my husband.

♦ Decide where I should live.

♦ Treat preachers in an unChrist-like manner. They would not treat the garbage collector the way some brethren speak to their brother in Christ who happens to be their preacher.

♦ Treat a preacher as a corporate employee.

♦ Tell us how to spend our salary.

♦ Ask a preacher's wife to work in order to supplement the family income. If you can't afford to or don't want to give him a raise, then admit it.

♦ Exalt the preacher's wife.

♦ Fail to respect family privacy.

♦ Consider her an *employee* of the church.

♦ Think of themselves above GOD.

♦ Expect the preacher and his family to live above what the Lord expects of them.

♦ Create a job description for the preacher's wife that is not found in Scripture.

It's always of interest to see how others look at the responsibilities of preaching. One congregation asked their young preacher to fill out a time sheet, recording the amount of time he worked. They wanted to make sure they were getting their money's worth. When the young man turned in the sheet, indicating much more than 40 hours of working time, was he compensated? I'll let you decide.

One young man, working with my husband for a period of time, was asked to help hang wallpaper—when he wasn't busy. I'm sure he would have been happy to help if needed, but the attitude displayed was, *he didn't have anything else to do.*

At one location, our experience was very pleasant for most of our time there. We enjoyed being with the brethren and experienced a good measure of personal growth while there. Good was done, there were lots of opportunities and many conversions; one of the most profitable works up until that time. Everything was going well until Satan stepped in and sent his influence. Under those circumstances, you may feel that you and your family are a dartboard—and a few of the members have the darts; and I hasten to say a few. Amid trials, it's easy to become so discouraged that we forget all the good there is around us. At times we have to remind ourselves and each other to focus! Focus on God's work; not on problems. Seek out those who are good and focus on doing good for others.

And when we think we've experienced it all, here comes something new.

It was during one such period of time that an older woman sought me out. When Frank would be out of town, she would call and ask if I wanted company. She knew I would be busy with homework and baths for the children, but she would bring her needlework and we would visit as we could. She was not there to discuss any current problems; in fact, it was never mentioned, but her support meant everything to me. To be guided by her influence was a memorable time for me and I came to deeply love and appreciate her.

When husbands are gone a lot, either because of demands of the local work or a meeting schedule, something is bound to break down! Fortunately, there are special brethren around who can aid us with such things. One Mr. Fix-it said, "You have to feel sorry for preachers. They don't know how to do anything but preach!" He was a jewel and often helped us with repairs and free advice on household things. It became a joke between my husband and me for a while because so many things happened when he was gone. A peeping tom invaded our neighborhood in the early years and even though blinds were closed, I could hear him at the bedroom window that summer night. Of course, the police were called, but it was the most frightening night I've ever spent, wondering how to protect myself and our two little boys. There was a strong temptation to get someone to stay with me during his next absence, but if I did, it would become more difficult to conquer that fear in the future. He, of certainty, will be away for periods of time. Is this character building?

Years later, our poor puppy had been poisoned, and died in my sweet little boy's arms on the way to the vet. Dad was gone. Actually, it was a teaching experience. My son was about to lose it, but I told him how much his help was needed and we both could cry later. Lesson? Face what you have to face; do what you have to do; collapse later. Personal milestones, accomplishments at school, maybe even birthdays will be while dad is gone. Gone. Did I mention gone? *It comes with the territory.*

Even though we had teased about his being gone, there came a time when the sting of being away was hard for both of us. Our lovely 19 year old daughter died very suddenly when my husband was in Romania; his first trip there. I was beside myself with concern for him, having to travel home alone with that knowledge. He deeply felt his absence at that time and hated that decisions had to be made without him. He was doing what he loves to do and had a part in teaching the very first convert in the city of Constanta. A church was eventually established there. Souls have been saved. How could I be hurt or angry about that? It's one of those rare things that come with the territory. It could happen to anyone. But we have a bonus. We have **always** been attended to by brethren, whatever the want or need, in times of unexpected accident or tragedy.

Even small things seem like big things when you must continually deal with them alone, but self-pity is never attractive and unresolved anger can lead to depression. There are solutions if staying home alone is a problem. Let it be known so others can help. I handled many things alone and now regret not asking for help. My stubborn independence didn't allow it, but looking back, others were robbed of the chance to come to my aid. Many are ready to help but they cannot read our minds or automatically know our needs. As time passes and we become more physically and spiritually mature, we'll be better equipped to handle difficult situations. Many occupations require travel and moving from place to place; not just preachers.

It is most comforting to know that others are lifting your name in prayer as these challenges are being faced. Anyone, at anytime can go to God in prayer—for any reason. Foolishly, prayer is often used as a last resort. If you're praying for someone in a difficult situation, let them know. The strength gained from prayer and daily reading centers us; helps us to endure trials and helps us to help others. Prayer can build friendships! When we share in the lives of others, they too share in our lives and give us strength. We're all working together for a common goal. Being able to share with, study with, and do daily things with other sisters are delightful things that come with the territory.

Now, on to more of the poll. We'll start with the hardest, and save the best for last.

The Hardest Thing about being a PW:

- ♦ Loneliness.
- ♦ Dealing with worldly brethren.
- ♦ Having to move and leave family and friends.
- ♦ Knowing at some point we'll move, dreading upheaval for the family.
- ♦ Getting attached and having to move; trying to develop new relationships with different people, all over again.
- ♦ Figuring out from one congregation to the next, how things work. Some groups like new thoughts and ideas and at some, new ideas are unwelcome. It's always a learning process but an insecure feeling; we feel like perpetual outsiders.
- ♦ Having to be *on* all the time.
- ♦ Being what I would like to be as a preacher's wife.
- ♦ Not being able to have close friends to confide in.
- ♦ Trying to be your best at all times and treat everyone alike.
- ♦ Having to learn dodging techniques when put on the spot by inquiring brethren so we won't be revealing information that has been entrusted to us.
- ♦ The *glass house* syndrome. Brethren can watch your every move, know your salary, rent, AC bills and every wrong answer your child got in class last Sunday. Zero privacy! It's difficult to reveal yourself to some brethren, knowing they can misconstrue what was said and turn it against you if they don't happen to like one of your husband's sermons. Some brethren want you to punch a time clock. Don't we wish we could! It would be nice to have only a 40 hour week. Who else is on call every day of the week? Even doctors can trade being on call.
- ♦ Having to say good-bye to God's people.
- ♦ Seeing people you have taught, worked with, or learned from fall away and be pulled back into the world or error.

Other areas of disappointment:

♦ I am disappointed that it takes a preacher's wife to try to get different cliques to socialize together. I wish brethren could try to get to know someone on the other side of the building.

♦ It's disappointing that brethren who have grown up in the same congregation don't appreciate the universal bond of Christians. Preaching families have to take the initiative to meet people and form relationships. Others don't appreciate the bond because they have never known what it is to rely on ONLY Christians when moving to a new town. They don't make the effort because they already have a set of friends at church and don't need any more.

♦ Why do I get phone calls from upset women wondering why I am mad at them? Why do they feel that I must invite everyone to a party that is not intended for their age group? One time, according to the caller, I just looked unhappy. I have never received such calls from neighbors or friends who do not know me as the preacher's wife.

♦ Is not my home *my* home? On one occasion, a sister told me that if I didn't intend to invite everyone to a shower, I shouldn't have one at all. That congregation had an unwritten rule that showers were only given for a first baby. Several friends decided to chip in for a stroller for a third time mother and have a little private party. I wouldn't dream of telling others whom they can invite into their homes. Do some sisters stay awake at night looking for things to criticize?

You can readily see that there are lots of areas in which the preacher and his wife need wisdom as well as self-control. Pray for the wisdom to handle situations in a way that will bring peace, aid spiritual growth, and bring glory to God.

The Best Thing about being a PW:

- ♦ Getting to know so many wonderful people in so many places.
- ♦ Association with many Christians, preachers, and elders.
- ♦ Being able to learn so much from my husband, as he has more time for study.
- ♦ The prayers of others who are supportive in your work.
- ♦ I get to travel with my husband and continue to listen to his good sermons.
- ♦ Being able to ask my husband at home and using lots of reference books.
- ♦ It's easy to make God and the brethren a priority. Our life naturally revolves around church life.
- ♦ It's encouraging to share hardships with other pw's. This too shall pass.
- ♦ Association with the best people on earth.
- ♦ Having a more flexible schedule than most. Preachers generally spend many more than 40 hours a week at their *job*. As they get older, children can even be taken on meetings and experience good things with their dad.
- ♦ Getting to know God's people.
- ♦ The number of fabulous, inspiring people you meet and have the privilege to learn from, enjoy, and mentor.
- ♦ Being loved by others in spite of your faults.

We, as preacher's wives, are so blessed! We've been able to associate with inspiring people and if I started naming . . . well, just have to mention a couple. The first preacher to stay in our home was Clinton Hamilton and I couldn't have been more nervous if he had been the pope! But he and I conspired together to trick Frank concerning what he was having for lunch one day, and I soon learned to be more comfortable. He just wanted to have a little fun. Eventually, we came to feel that if we weren't able to keep the preacher for some reason, the week was incomplete! It's not always easy for a man to spend a busy week in a household with four children, but we shared in each other's lives for that time, getting to *pick his brain* and discuss important issues. We were friends when they left and they had been an inspiration; an influence for good in our lives.

James R. Cope stayed in our home several times. One time he gave some special attention to our youngest son, who, at the time, was having some learning problems. They bonded during the week, and when it was time to say good-bye, our sweet little boy cried, hating to see him go. An earlier time, he gave my discouraged husband some advice that has never been forgotten. "You don't build anything—a church, a marriage—anything, by majoring on its weak points." We were letting a few cantankerous brethren color our outlook! I say we, because it's *our* work. He was hired, not me, but it's still our work. My task is to help him accomplish his goals; to provide for his needs so he can stay focused. Being a preacher's wife has helped me beyond measure. Learning from my good husband is a plus. He studies more now than ever; has a dogged persistence, not only in teaching, but in strengthening the saved; *loves* to sit across the table to study with someone. Early on I learned being flexible was important because if he can study with someone, he'll do it. His books and outlines are in his car at all times and has been known to approach someone and study on the spot. We can make or break our husbands, especially in the way we face our duties at home. If we are unorganized and flighty, he will of necessity need to spend time making up for that; time that he could have used more profitably. Could Satan use me as a tool for discouraging my husband?

Time passes and new challenges arise. The first time I taught a ladies class, I went home and took a nerve pill. It's not easy to put yourself out there, but as the years creep up, we who qualify as *older* need to be teaching! How can we refuse the opportunity? Will we stand before God and hand him an undeveloped talent? What better way to glorify God and present our bodies as a living sacrifice? 1 Corinthians 6:20; Romans 12:1.

If I could have known then what is known now, what would I be doing in preparation?

+ Find an effective plan for Bible study and then study it! (Gather your tools: Bible, *Vine's Expository Dictionary*, concordance, atlas and reliable commentary.) Prepare to teach—then do it. Find a mentor who can inspire you.

+ Knowing the Word is an advantage—in anything you do. Hint: Pick a subject. Dwell on it. Daily read from Scripture whatever you can about the subject. When in the car, doctor's office, etc. meditate on it and from memory, try to find illustrations. Make notes from sermons and classes. You'll be surprised how that subject will develop.

Even small things seem like big things when you must continually deal with them alone.

+ The Bible itself is a good counseling tool, but prepare as you can to counsel others, especially in marriage and parenting.

+ Study elements of writing. There is a tremendous need for good workbooks for women as well as curriculum for our children's Bible classes. If you've ever tried to plan a quarter on evidences for children, you'll quickly agree.

+ Preaching is a daunting responsibility. Pray often for guidance.

+ Rest. Jesus needed time away to rest—away from the people. Preachers' wives have a high incidence of stress related health issues.

Years ago, Frank and I stayed with an elderly couple during a meeting in Florida. Their old country home was on an island and the house was built by slave labor in the late 1800s. They were a delightful couple and showed us many interesting items they had collected through the years. As he showed us around the property, he commented on planting trees here and there as he wanted to maintain its natural properties. He said, "I'll never live to see them grow, but at least they will be there for the next person." In the next section, you'll find articles written by good women, preachers' wives of a generation now gone. By their lives and by their writings, they left a great legacy for others; for us. I've never forgotten the conversation with that old man, so I'm asking—what legacy will you leave for the generation of preacher's wives that follow? For what will you be praying as you conclude this book? We serve under a different set of circumstances, but we want to serve to the fullest—and *finish strong.*

"A good name is to be more desired than great wealth, favor is better than silver and gold," Proverbs 22:1.

Appendix A:
The Preacher's Wife
Mrs. James P. (Bobbie) Miller
Published in Searching the Scriptures, Probably in the '50s

By no stretch of the imagination would I consider myself an authority on what is desired of a Preacher's Wife simply because I was invited to share with you some insight nineteen years of being one has given to me. I do believe, however, that by thinking together we may come to more fully understand and appreciate the great scope of the happy and profitable life of a preacher and his family—much of which depends upon the preacher's wife.

The wife was created of man to be a helpmeet for him, Genesis 2:20. In order to truly be a helpmeet, she must then be *one flesh* with her husband, and only upon a full and complete understanding of the scope of his work could one hope to be a good help meet, *one flesh*, with a preacher husband. Therefore, our first task is to call to mind some of the things required of a preacher. The commission under which he labors is, *"Go ye therefore, and teach all nations, baptizing them in the name of the Father, and of the Son and of the Holy Spirit: Teaching them to observe all things whatsoever I have commanded you; and lo, I am with you always, even unto the end of the world,"* (Matthew 28:19, 20) or as Mark records it, *"preach the gospel to every creature."* He then, is to teach and preach wherever he can most profitably work. How could he be free to do this though, if his *so called* help meet refuses to live more than twenty miles from her mother?

In some ways a preacher's work might be likened to that of a doctor in that each is a life dedicated to **service**. A doctor's work is one of service to humanity—to save their physical bodies of misery and suffering. A gospel preacher helps relieve needs of the physical body, but in addition, administers to the spiritual needs of humanity. His service, then, is two-fold—to man and to God. What higher, more noble calling could one seek than this place of service in helping man save his soul in this life and the life hereafter. The Bible recognizes this to be true, *"How beautiful are the feet of them that preach the gospel of peace, and bring glad tidings of good things,"* Romans 10:15. As a mother with a pain-racked baby breathes a prayer of thanksgiving when she hears the sure steps of the feet of the doctor as he comes up the walk to heal her sick child, so those who are racked with sin say how beautiful are the feet of the one who administers the saving gospel to them. We as women cannot aspire to be preachers, matters not how noble a work it may be, for such is forbidden by the things bound by Paul. But what more noble service could a woman aspire to than that of becoming a helpmeet to a gospel preacher? A preacher's work is a selfless work, one which requires its master to give rather than receive, or that of putting the needs of another before self.

Now, having set forth the work of a preacher, we then can better understand what would be expected of his helpmeet. We know that the man and wife are to become *one flesh*, that is, one in purpose, interests, desires and a mutual sharing of love and work toward a common goal. If the husband is a gospel preacher and his life is dedicated to **service** to others, so too, if they are one flesh, must his wife dedicate herself to service—to husband, to children, to God, and to all humanity. What a big order this surely must be! The important thing is to keep her eyes set on the common goal, willing always to do that which is necessary to reach it. This means that we as preachers' wives must be as selfless as must be the preacher. One of the first and hardest lessons for such a wife is that her husband's time is not always at her disposal. There may be times when he needs to be away from home—yes, helping others, when you feel lonely and need him yourself. Especially is this true if he is an evangelist spending much time away in meetings. Evening, approaching night, twilight, is a happy time of the day and I like to think of it as a time when families gather in from busy day's activities and share their experiences. After the dinner dishes are finished, how pleasant it is if the family can go to sit on the front porch as twilight falls and share in pleasant communion with each other, neighbors, and nature's early evening panorama. But for a preacher's family there are few such evenings, and with the falling of twilight is the falling of loneliness as a covering for the wife left to keep *home fires burning.* I early found this experience a place to make adjustment and lift again my eyes to the mission of service. Likewise, special days—anniversaries, birthdays, yes even the birth of our own children are joys meant to be shared by husband and wife though we may not always find it so. Our only child was born in Philadelphia, 1100 miles from my home, while my husband was preaching and saving souls in a meeting in Detroit, Michigan. However, a good preacher's wife must be cheerful that she may encourage her husband in his work and understand its demands on his time and attention, never nagging or demanding too much of him. There is no room for self pity and regrets over *what might have been.*

But let us here point up some of the many wonderful and abundant advantages to be found in being a preacher's wife. She is blessed above all others with family and friends—whole congregations are her brothers and sisters in the Lord. She enjoys the admiration and esteem of all those with whom she is associated. What ends people of this world would go to, to gain a measure of the esteem and recognition that is that of a preacher's wife. She is appreciated and loved for the good work that she does—grant that she seek always to conduct herself in such a manner as to be worthy of this esteem, not expecting it merely because she is a preacher's wife. She is fortunate also in that her associates are of the finest, highest type people on earth. She is not of the drunken brawl and base living, low moral type people. Her associates are of higher intellectual accomplishments, lives in atmosphere of books, cultural activities, and broadening experiences in travels. Hers can be the very best and highest type of circumstances on earth. What is more, she enjoys the security and peace of mind knowing of the daily partitions [sic] of the members of the congregation on her behalf. What other kind of wife would be half so fortunate and blessed?

Let us now see if we can put together a composite picture of a good preacher's wife. First, she must recognize and respect the fact that the husband is head of the wife (Ephesians 5:23) and that she is to submit herself unto him, Ephesians 5:22. I am troubled to hear girls, perhaps teasingly, say that they would not be willing to promise to *obey* in the marriage ceremony. Surely such is lightly spoken, for how could we hope to exemplify the teaching of the Word if we would be unwilling to recognize the husband as head of the wife. Perhaps it but speaks her lack of complete trust in him, fearing that he would or could expect things unreasonable of her by such a promise. However, we are assured that *"so ought men to love their wives as their own bodies…*(Ephesians 5:28), *for no man every yet hated his own flesh."* Upon mutual trust in this principle, who then would be unwilling and afraid to promise to obey?

Furthermore, a good preacher's wife is a good mother, bringing up children to respect and honor the work their father is doing. This could scarcely be true if the only reason for denying them certain activities is that they are a preacher's child. Such would but drive them to resent, yea, hate the fact that their father was a preacher.

She is affectionate, well-adjusted, adaptable, possesses a desire to grow and mature with her husband. Her background is similar to her husband's environment, tastes, and education. Ideally, she is college trained and has had some business experience. She is an intelligent listener when her husband shares his problems and experiences with her. When asked, she offers her objective counsel and viewpoint. She never commits the unpardonable act of betraying a confidence her husband has shared. It even means that every member of the congregation is treated alike, showing no favorites, choosing no special confidantes. Members of a congregation like to feel there are no favorites with the preacher's wife. Good business for the smart wife is to see that they live within his income. Together, they will plan the general outlay of the budget and cheerfully accept that as a challenge to her best efforts. It may mean that

fine silver, china, and expensive clothes will not be hers, but what difference does that make if she knows and understands what she is looking
for in life. Skill in sewing and home economics, hence, are a vital part of
her training before marriage.

And if all that were not enough, she will still need to be a maid,
the chauffeur, nurse, a secretary, a handy man, laundress, governess,
educator, and willing and able to entertain hospitable anyone at most any
time.

We have included only some of the more essential outlines in our
picture of the preacher's wife. The filling in of the details will be different
with each person, but then we aren't seeking to make a stereotype. What
we are is simply an outward expression of inner attitudes and ideals and
it would be difficult to *change* ourself or order ourself to be that that be-
fits a preacher's wife simply because we decided to be one without firmly
believing every precept we would live by. To be a good preacher's wife,
then, *should* call for no change of behavior on our part. I like to think
that I am the same as if I were a plumber's wife. It, like that of an elder, is
an office to be desired. I am thankful that in the providence of God I am
privileged to be a preacher's wife. I would not change it if I could. I would
like to believe often I am a help and seldom a hindrance to my husband's
work, and will say with Ruth, "*Whither thou goest, I will go; and whither
thou lodgest, I will lodge; thy people shall be my people, and thy God my
God: Where thou diest, will I die, and there will I be buried; the Lord do so
to me, and more also, if ought but death part thee and me.*"

If I can but inspire you to desire to be the true helpmeet a
preacher must have to do his work with joy and thanksgiving, then will
I count with gladness every minute of the time away from my family tonight. With apologies to Kipling's IF:

A Preacher's Wife

If she can devote a selfless life and not a martyr be,

If she can live a righteous life and not feel self-righteously,

If she can be a friend to *all* not choosing any more near and dear,

If she can find joy in others joy and weep with them in tear,

If she can look to treasures stored above and not the earthly
       things of life,

Then, my ladies, she is a jewel much to be admired as a
       Preacher's Wife.

Appendix B:
The Blessings of Being a Preacher's Wife
by Barbara C. Adams

Originally published in Truth Magazine, March 22, 1973 anonymously
Republished in Searching the Scriptures, March 1978
Republished in an abridged form in Biblical Insights, October 2006

Tonight is the 23rd of December. In another week a new year will be upon us. It, naturally, is a time for reflection and a time to count our blessings. We are blessed because we live in America and are free to worship God in the way He commanded us; we are blessed because we have plenty to eat and warm houses in which to live while people in other parts of the world are starving. But there is one blessing that I share with a relative few in this world. It is a blessing that I prize very highly and one that I am thankful God gave me the freedom and opportunity to choose—I am blessed in that I chose to become a preacher's wife.

I can almost hear some now saying: "That's a strange thing to say. She must be off her rocker in some way. A preacher's wife can't be thankful or call that a blessing. Why she is often criticized and put on the spot. Her husband is often gone for days at a time and she is alone. Her children are in the spotlight and their actions minutely inspected. Preachers never make much money or have fine houses. They must move every so often. How can she call that a blessing?"

Yes, I can hear all these comments, even though unspoken. And I grant that most of them are true. But I still count it a blessing. Until recently, I never gave it much thought. I just went along from day to day doing what had to be done. However, some recent events have prompted me to reflect on this blessing. Perhaps my reflections can help a few others to appreciate their lot in life a little more and also cause others to choose this way, if the choice presents itself.

Recently, I have heard some voice the opinion that they did not want to be a preacher's wife or that they did not want their girl to become a preacher's wife. I have heard of boys who want to give up preaching because their sweethearts did not want to be preachers' wives. You know, I never gave that a whole lot of thought. Maybe my mother wishes I had; but if so, she never spoke that thought. She did tell me that she wanted me to help make my husband a good one. Those of you who know him can judge how well I succeeded!

What is the life of a preacher's wife really like? There are others who have been *at it* far longer than I and who could tell far more about it, I am sure; but tonight let me give you some of my thoughts.

It will soon be twenty-eight years since I decided to take that *giant step* and I never have been sorry for one minute. It has not always been smooth sailing or an easy course to follow. I have made a lot of mistakes—for these, I am truly sorry—but God forgives a preacher's wife on the same basis He forgives anyone else. The brethren where we have lived have *put up with*, encouraged, laughed, and even cried with us on various occasions. For this, I am grateful. Without their help, I never could have *made it*, I suppose.

I do not believe that I was consciously trained to become a preacher's wife. However, I never was discouraged. It just never really concerned me too much one way or the other. We had preachers in our family (though all are either dead or liberal now), and when we could all get together, it was a wonderful time. I am sure that when I left to go to Florida College in 1949 the thought must have occurred to my parents that I might marry a preacher, since that institution was (and is) well known for the marriages that are created there. I am an *only child* and when I left for college it was for good, except for short, infrequent visits. That is not the way I would like for it to be. However, because of our work it has had to be like that. So being an only child is no excuse for not becoming a preacher's wife.

Next week is the twentieth birthday of our older son. Some of you will remember where he was born. Not in some comfortable American hospital in my hometown, to be sure. No, he was born in a University hospital in Bergen, Norway, thousands of miles from either of our homes and parents, with a doctor who was a Communist and nurses and attendants who did not speak or understand English.

It was not an easy time. We had few friends there then, having been in Norway only four months. At the time, I came as close to not caring about anything as I ever have. But I thank God that I did not entirely give in. Even then I did not regret being a preacher's wife. What I am saying is this: There may be times when you, as a preacher's wife, will have to leave this country. It is almost a certainty that you will have to leave your hometown and parents. But as Jesus said in Luke 14:26—"*If any man cometh unto me, and hateth not his father, and mother, and wife, and children, and brethren, and sisters, yea, and his own life also, he cannot be my disciple.*"

This is a time of protest and discontent. The younger generations are critics of the older generation. They say we are materialistic. But I just wonder what it is when a boy decides not to preach because the girl he wants to marry just does not want to move around every so often, or does not want to leave her parents or her hometown. She wants the security of a job and a house in one locality all her life. Is this materialism? What else?

Preacher's wives are not a special breed. Why, God did not even give us special admonitions as he did the wives of elders and deacons. We have the same admonitions as all other women. However, there are a few commands which certainly pertain to a preacher's wife.

As with other Christians, we dare not to gossip or bear tales. No Christian should do this. And Certainly not a preacher's wife. She is in a position to know things about other Christians which do not need to be made public. Things are said to her and her husband in confidence and she needs to be able to keep such knowledge to herself, lest it hurt the person, her husband, and even the congregation. In fact, some things her husband should not even tell her. If I had any one piece of advice to give any girl who is about to marry a preacher, it would be, *Keep your mouth shut!* Neither is it her business to advertise decisions that the elders make, or, for that matter, to try to tell the elders or her husband which decisions to make.

And which of us has not at some time engaged in a little self-pity? Some are more prone to this than others. But a Christian has no right or need to do this. We are called to serve God wherever and whenever we can. The preacher's wife cannot afford self-pity. There will often be times when her husband will be called away to the hospital to sit with a family during an operation, or to a funeral home after a sudden death, or to a person's home during a trying time when a marriage is on the brink of failure, or even to a local jail to help somebody in trouble. She must wait at home with a supper pushed to the back of the stove or in the oven. Or he may be gone for several days at a time in a gospel meeting clear across the country, or to a lectureship, or to a debate. Maybe he will even be involved in his work half-way around the world.

I have never asked my husband not to go where he thought he was needed for God's work. Yet I must confess that I came close in 1971 when he and J. T. Smith decided to go to the Philippine Islands. I knew there would be physical danger involved in such a trip; it would mean that the children and I would be alone for an entire month. What if one of the children got seriously ill? Or what if I became sick? However, I agreed that he should go. In fact, I knew he would go before he even finished telling me of the need. For some reason, I've always believed that it was up to me to let him go and that it was up to God to take care of him.

So far, it has worked out that way. How glad I am now that he and brother Smith went. Because of their efforts and the efforts of others who have gone, the brethren there have been helped immensely. By mail, I have come to know many of those people. They have had many difficulties and troubles which many of us would find unbearable. Would I be willing for him to go again? You bet I would!

Congregations often expect too much of the preacher's wife. They seem to think that for some reason they *own* her and should be able to tell her what to do and how to do it. This attitude can cause problems. Let me hurriedly and thankfully say that I have never really faced this problem. The congregations where we have worked have been very considerate along this line; but I do know that such things have happened. Just because the church owns the house in which the preacher lives or pays the rent for him does not give the members the right to tell the wife how to run her house. This is their home for the time that they live there.

Neither does the congregation *hire* the preacher's wife. For the first twenty years we were married, I did a lot of secretarial work for my husband and the church. I knew how to do such work and was glad to do it. With one exception, I have never been paid for such work. However, a congregation has no right to expect more from a preacher's wife along this line than from any other woman in the congregation. A preacher is not always as well paid as some in this life. He does not have many fringe benefits which workers in plants or offices have. Few churches pay social security, health insurance premiums, or pension plans. Yet, I do not know of many churches that will deny a preacher an extra day off at a holiday season or fail to continue his salary during a long, drawn-out illness. Though your daughter may not always have the *most* in this life, you can rest assured that there are fringe benefits which few others will ever have.

What am I talking about? For one thing: friends. Yes, our friends . . . from Maine to California; Washington to Florida; in Canada, Norway and the Philippines. We would not trade these acquaintances for any amount of money on earth. These are people with whom we have worked through the years and who now have scattered around the country and the world. They include preachers, and, yes, their wives. They include sons and daughters of preachers who have grown up and married in the past few years. Whole congregations are included. These are all brothers and sisters in Christ, and all of them are (or should be) striving toward the same goal—an eternal home in heaven. These friends are the finest people on earth.

These *preacher-wife* years have meant a broader education for my children and me than would have been possible had we always lived in the same place. How else could we have seen the midnight sun of Norway; the snow of northeast Ohio; the blastoff of a rocket at Cape Kennedy; the rock-bound coast of Maine; the lakes of Ontario; the cathedral of Worms, Germany where Martin Luther took his stand? I do not mean for this to sound as if we have been to these places just for the fun of traveling. That is not it at all. The work came first and that is what took us to these places, but I would be foolish to let you think that it did not benefit our lives. It has even helped our children in their school work.

One of the greatest fringe benefits is being the constant recipients of the prayers of the congregation. Who else has God's blessing invoked upon them in public prayers as much as the preacher and his family? Most of all, a preacher's wife develops a better understanding of people and a desire to have a part in the saving of their souls. Who could describe the frame of mind a preacher is in after someone has obeyed the gospel, or a wayward church member has repented, or some evidence is seen of good resulting from your husband's efforts? Could it just be that I did have some part in making that possible? If so, then it has been worth it after all.

—{ *Permission has been granted by Connie Adams & Wilson Adams to reprint the article written by Bobbie Adams.* }—

Appendix C

The following is part of an interview of Mrs. Irven Lee, author of *Mrs. Lee's Stories about Jesus* and *Mrs. Lee's Stories about God's First People*, conducted by Donnie Rader and printed in *Guardian of Truth,* March 1995. Permission to reprint granted by Mrs. Lee's daughter, Sandra Waldron.

Life as a Preacher's Wife

How long were you married?

Fifty-five years.

How did you build a love that lasted 55 years? What's the key?

Well, I never gave that any thought. We never considered divorce. Murder, yes, but not divorce. I married knowing this is for life. You've got to make the best of it, good or bad. This idea that people live together for 55 years and never have any cross words or disagreements? I think that's foolish. If that's true, there is one of them that has no mind of his own. We were both interested in the same things. We were interested in spiritual things. It's easier to build a life on spiritual values than it is on worldly things.

How would you describe your life as a preacher's wife?

It isn't an easy life. Preachers live in fish bowls. Everything you do, everything you say is under scrutiny. Everybody knows what's going on in your home. You simply have to live with that in mind always. There's no privacy in a preacher's life actually. But it can be a very rewarding life. I'm certainly thankful that I was married to a preacher. I am a much better person because of having lived with a preacher.

What advice would you give to a young wife whose husband is thinking about preaching?

Make up your mind to be content. I think one of the problems with preachers' wives is that they cannot adjust to the lack of roots. There is not much chance to put down roots and have a real solid foundation under you. You have to learn to be content with what life metes out to you. So you make up your mind . . . if Paul could learn to be content in all that he suffered, I can too. I was accused one time of thinking that when Paul said, "whatsoever state I am in therein to be content" that he meant the state of the Union I am in, I'll be therein content or in whatever situation of life I'll be content. And be a supporter of your husband's work. Never criticize your husband to someone else. If he just makes a flop on a sermon sometime, you talk to him at home about it. But don't dare talk to somebody else that you think he just flopped tonight. Completely support him. It's sometimes hard, but it can be done.

How did you contribute to brother Lee's work as a preacher?

I think one of the greatest things I did for him was just helping him in his speaking. He had the knowledge. In school he majored in math and science. He didn't know what sentence construction meant. He said, "If you don't know English, the best thing to do is to marry an English major." So when we first married he said, "I know I don't use good grammar. I don't use good sentence structure. Will you help me in that?" So his having asked me to do it, then I was perfectly free to point out any of his mistakes. I worked with him on his oral speaking. Then, when he began his writing, he knew nothing about writing. But he knew what he wanted to say. So I would take what he wanted to say and help him put it into the proper words.

What about later in life as he preached, other than encouragement, were there other things you did that you felt contributed to his success in his work?

I kept the home fires burning to relieve him of as many of the home duties as I could to give him full-time to preaching. I was the one that kept the things running at home. That's an important part because his mind was so absorbed with his work. And he did so much preaching that he didn't have time for the things at home. Well, I never expected him to do those things. That was my work. And I relieved him of as much of it as I could.

How have you adjusted to being a widow?

Simply making up my mind I will be content. Now, it has been terribly hard. The first summer I just think of it as that terrible summer. But it was a matter of "I will do it. Others have done it. I can." It has been just sheer determination. I'm not going to be miserable the rest of my life. He would not have wanted me to spend my life grieving. I'm not going to. And I have wrapped myself completely in my classes.

Role as a Mother

Was raising your children in a preacher's family more difficult than for other mothers?

I've been told many times that is more difficult. Now, I don't know. I've never tried any other situation. But I had only daughters and very obedient daughters. They were both easily trained. I never had big problems. My little girls and I spent 24 hours a day together. We were talking together. We were doing things together. I taught them deep respect for their father. What he says; this is law. This is order. I taught them that they must keep in mind that your father is in the public. The world sees everything that he does. Whatever you do is going to reflect on him. Therefore, you live a model life so that your life doesn't reflect on his work.

What would you tell a man and his wife or a mother about raising children? What kind of advice would you give to a young couple starting a family?

Keep a close, close relationship with them. Start early teaching them Bible stories. The constant association with your children I think is such an important thing. Don't ever let them get out from under your influence. Know what your children are doing. Know always where your children are. And let them know always where you are. So there is constant communication.

How have you been successful in passing the gospel on to your children?

They just never knew anything else. I brought them up the way I was brought up. They don't know when they started hearing these stories. They were too young. And then just constant, constant talking. There was never time for other things. Sandra used to say, "Children say, 'I don't have anything to do.' When do they have time to look for something to do?" Our time was so full. We went to so many services in which my husband preached.

How does the family unit differ from earlier days?

There is no unity now. Each one goes his own separate way. There is so little home life. Very few families actually sit down together and eat meals together. They are so busy in the morning. Half the families don't even eat breakfast. If they do, they just eat it on the run. There is no social life in the family. There is no visiting together. This one doesn't know what that one is doing. And families are so separated now that we've lost the influence of the older generation on the younger ones. They are not together.

What's your perception of the day-care centers?

I have very, very little use for the average day-care center. It is a necessary part of our modem society, I suppose. But there is a grave danger in it. The children end up not even knowing their own parents. And since they don't know their parents, their parents don't know them. They are closer to the one who cares for them in the day care centers than they are their parents. But I'm not qualified to actually talk about them because I don't know much about them. But I'm just seeing some of the product that comes out. I appreciate godly women who keep children in their homes and are trying to influence some for good. But I think the average day-care center is a detriment to the family.

What guidelines would you give parents with teen-agers entering the dating years?

That's such a bad time. If they have waited until they are teen-agers and ready to date before they do much instructing on the matter, well they've waited entirely too late. The instruction on dating should start when they are old enough to know anything at all. Children should be taught, "Now you're going to be Christians and you must associate, as near as possible, with Christians. And you are to marry Christians." Now, that doesn't guarantee in our modern society that they will have good homes all their lives, because we're seeing so many Christian homes breaking up. But if you start off with too many strikes against you, why it's hard to deal with . . . the more you have in common the better.

My mother always said you're not going to marry one that you never date. Therefore, you date only one that there would be no sin in your marrying. You cannot date one who has been married. In fact, she had married out of the church. She knew the heartaches connected with that. She absolutely forbade one of her daughters to date a non-Christian.

Role of Women

What changes have you seen in the role of women through the years?

This just feeling like "I want to be more a part of things. This home life is not for me. I don't want to be tied down in the home. I want a job. I want a career."

And it's the wanting to get away from what our poor mothers had to do: "Our poor mothers were just tied down at home. They didn't have the opportunities that I have, so they missed out on so many things. And I want something better. I don't know why I ought to have to do everything at home. My husband is just as capable of doing those things as I am. Why shouldn't he take his share of the work in the house? Why are some things women's work? Why does he think that I have to cook the meals and wash the dishes? Why can't he do those things? Why do I have to do all the care for the children? They are just as much his as they are mine."

I think we are forgetting the importance of being women. We've forgotten that a woman was the crowning act of God's creation. We've forgotten that God honored the woman as a woman. And we think that the only way that we can be of any importance is to get out here and do what the men are doing. This submissive role that we are told we must observe; that is so repulsive!

We have failed to teach our children to be ladies and that there is an honor in being a woman. And now, instead of giving our little girls baby dolls to play with, we give them Barbie dolls. We give them the teenagers. And we teach them to keep the hair of their dolls. We teach them that this Barbie doll now has a career. And we've forgotten the little baby doll that has to be babied and petted and put to bed at night and kissed and loved. We're not teaching them to be mothers. We're not teaching them to love little children.

How do you view subjection to a man? Did you ever view that as being inferior?

Oh no! It's so wonderful to have somebody make the decisions. My husband was the public one. He took care of me. He provided for me. I didn't have to make those major decisions. The submission was simple; I had somebody to take care of me. To be submissive has been such a wonderful thing for me.

How do you respond to those women who act as if there is nothing they can do in the church?

I'd say that you have a private role. You can teach your children. You can teach your friends. But your work is not the public work. Why should you want it to be? I can't understand women wanting it; women in business meetings. Why on earth would a woman want to be there? Why do you want the public life? In your private life you can do an awful lot of teaching.

Why do you think women are wanting to teach men and be in business meetings, etc.?

I think it's the influence of the women's liberation movement that Christian women have unconsciously allowed to creep into their lives. They are hearing it on every side. Everything is geared to that now. Our young people are hearing this in the school, on the radio and on television that the woman must fulfill her potential; that she is just as capable as the man. So she must fulfill her potential. In so many cases, the women have more Bible knowledge because they've had more time to spend in Bible study. They think, "If I've got more Bible knowledge, why shouldn't I get up here and teach these men?"

I think it is the woman's liberation movement. We've been so influenced even in the church beyond what we'd like to admit.

What kind of things have you done in the kingdom or the service of the Lord?

Of course, you know about my little Bible story books. I wrote them when my children were the age for them. I wrote them as a challenge. I told my husband, "There are no Bible stories books for children that are worth reading." My husband then said, "Write something."

Then, I began teaching the classes. The classes have been the main things that I have contributed to the work, whatever value they have been. I taught children's classes until I was middle age. There is nothing I enjoy more now than teaching ladies classes. I've taught various kinds. The kind I like to teach is simply teaching Bible topics or teaching the book of John, the book of Acts, etc. I've done a lot of teaching on the role of women in the home and the godly woman. Last year in the Vacation Bible School I took a different approach and taught a series of lessons on the "Ungodly Woman and Her Deadly Influence." That was very effective I felt. My classes have been strictly Bible.

Comment on the kind of things you did while brother Lee traveled in meetings. I understand you taught some classes.

Yes, I did often do that. I would often have, during the week, five lessons for women. In many of these classes I did teach on the home.

Did you help with the Use Your Bible series?

No, I did not. Now, I wrote some workbooks for women. They were just O. T. women and N. T. women. They were introductions and questions.

What kind of things can a woman do in the kingdom without violating the role that God has given her?

Aside from her teaching, there is hospitality to be extended. That's a very important part in a woman's work of opening her home to others and inviting in and being available in cases of sickness. Being there in case of a young woman's sickness; being able to care for her children for her. Providing food. Just being there when a friend is in trouble. Be available for encouragement to others.

Why do you think we have less hospitality among the brethren than in times past?

We're too busy. So many of the problems that are in the church today are simply because we're living in an age when everybody is so busy. There is the breakdown in the family unit so that the family itself doesn't eat together. Therefore, we don't invite visitors in. It is too great an effort to fix a meal in the house. So if we invite someone, we more often take him to a restaurant. So we lose this sense of hospitality. We have just forgotten how much encouragement there is to the family itself in having someone in your home.

More Bible workbooks that you can order from Spiritbuilding.com or your favorite Christian bookstore.

BIBLE STUDIES

Inside Out (Carl McMurray)
Studying spiritual growth in bite sized pieces

Night and Day (Andrew Roberts)
Comparing N.T. Christianity and Islam

We're Different Because..., w/Manual (Carl McMurray)
A workbook on authority and recent church history

From Beneath the Altar (Carl McMurray)
A workbook commentary on the book of Revelation

1 & 2 Timothy and Titus (Matthew Allen)
A workbook commentary on these letters from Paul

The Parables, Taking a Deeper Look (Kipp Campbell)
A relevant examination of our Lord's teaching stories

The Minor Prophets, Vol. 1 & 2, w/PowerPack (Matthew Allen)
Old lessons that speak directly to us today

Esteemed of God, the Book of Daniel, w/Manual (Carl McMurray)
Covering the man as well as the time between the testaments

Faith in Action: Studies in James (Mike Wilson)
Bible class workbook and commentary on James

The Lion is the Lamb (Andrew Roberts)
Study of the King of Kings, His glorious kingdom, & His promised return

Church Discipline, w/Manual (Royce DeBerry)
A quarter's study on an important task for the church

Communing with the Lord (Matthew Allen)
A study of the Lord's Supper and issues surrounding it

Seeking the Sacred (Chad Sychtysz)
How to know God the way that HE wants us to know Him

1 Corinthians & 2 Corinthians study workbooks (Chad Sychtysz)
Detailed studies to take the student through these important letters

Living a Spirit Filled Life, w/PowerPack (Matthew Allen)
An overview study of Galatians & Ephesians with practical applications

From Fear to Faith (Matthew Allen)
A study to build a greater assurance of personal salvation

Behind the Preacher's Door (Warren Berkley, editor)
A call to personal purity for preachers & all Christians

The AD 70 Doctrine (Morris Bowers)
A study of this false and growing doctrine of men

The Last Mile of the Way (Kipp Campbell)
An examination of the last week of Christ's life on earth

TEENS/YOUNG ADULTS

Transitions, w/PowerPack (Ken Weliever)
A relevant life study for this changing age group
Snapshots: Defining Moments in a Girl's Life (Nicole Sardinas)
How to make godly decisions when it really matters
The Path of Peace (Cassondra Givans)
Relevant and important topics of study for teens
The Purity Pursuit (Andrew Roberts)
Helping teens achieve purity in all aspects of life
The Gospel and You (Andrew Roberts)
Thirteen weeks of daily lessons for Jr High and High School ages
Paul's Letter to the Romans (Matthew Allen)
Putting righteousness by faith on an understandable level
God's Plan for Dating and Marriage (Dennis Tucker)
A look at some pitfalls to avoid during dating & a study of marriage.
Eye to Eye with Women of the Bible (Joanne Beckley)
A workbook for teen girls

WOMEN

Reveal In Me... (Jeanne Sullivan)
A ladies study on finding and developing one's own talents
I Will NOT Be Lukewarm, w/PowerPack (Dana Burk)
A ladies study on defeating mediocrity
Will You Wipe My Tears? (Joyce Jamerson)
Resources to teach us how to help others through sorrow
Bridges or Barriers, w/Manual (Cindy DeBerry/Angie Kmitta)
Study encouraging harmony with younger/older sisters-in-Christ
Learning to Sing at Midnight (Joanne Beckley)
A study book about spiritual growth benefiting women of all ages
Forgotten Womanhood (Joanne Beckley)
Workbook which covers purity of purpose in serving God
Re-charging Your Prayer Life (Lonnie Cruse)
Workbook for any woman wanting a richer prayer life
Heading for Harvest (Joyce Jamerson)
A study to help ladies digest the fruit of the Spirit
Does This Armor Make Me Look Fat? (Lonnie Cruse)
A study of Ephesians 6:10-18 for women

PERSONAL GROWTH
Compass Points (Carl McMurray)
22 foundation lessons for home studies or new Christians
Marriage Through the Ages, w/Manual (Royce & Cindy DeBerry)
A quarter's study of God's design for this part of our life
Parenting Through the Ages, w/Manual (Royce & Cindy DeBerry)
Bible principles tested and explained by successful parents
What Should I Do?, w/Manual (Dennis Tucker)
A study that seeks Bible answers to life's important questions
When Opportunity Knocks, w/Manual (Matthew Allen)
Lessons on how to meet the JW/Mormon who knock on your door

SPECIAL INTERESTS
In the Eye of the Hurricane - AUTISM (Juli Liske)
A family's journey from the shock of an autistic diagnosis to victory
I Cried Out, You Answered Me - DEPRESSION (Sheree McMillen)
What happens when faith and depression live in the same home
Her Little Soldier - DIABETES (Craig Dehut)
The journey of a young man suffering from Type 1 Juvenile Diabetes
For However Brief a Time (Warren Berkley)
A son's human interest tales of his father in a time now gone by
Family Bible Study Series (Ken Weliever)
A series of 16 quarters of Bible class curriculum ideas

JUST FOR KIDS
Greta's Purpose (Rebecca Helvey)
A children's book about a Great Dane who struggles with fitting in
Rudy's Path (Rebecca Helvey)
A story of a chocolate colored dog who finds belief, a family, and a name
Gus and Phil Stories Audio CDs (Ivan Benson)
Stories of true friendship and Christian values
Spiritbuilding Bible Challenge on CD (Mark Hudson, Alayne Hunt)
An entertaining CD-ROM series of Bible questions & answers
Bucky Beaver (Julie Robbins)
Children's book which teaches biblical lessons of obedience & diligence

*All PowerPacks include PowerPoint presentations +
Teacher's Manual

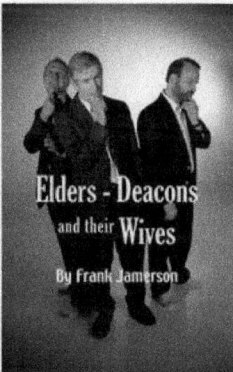

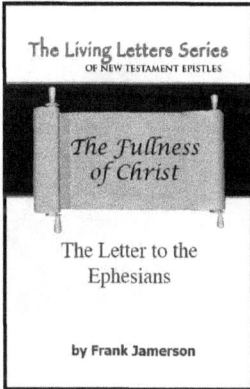

For Kid's Only

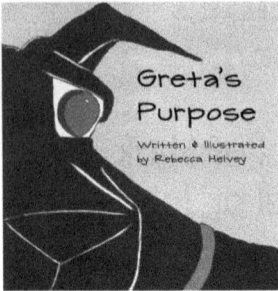

Greta's Purpose: A children's book about a Great Dane who struggles with fitting in.

Rudy's Path: The follow-up to Greta's Purpose is a story of a chocolate colored dog who, after losing faith, finds belief, a family, and a name.

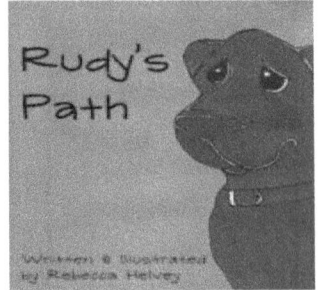

Gus and Phil Stories Audio CDs: "In the Beginning" is a story that reminds us of the power of true friendship. "The Baseball Toss" shows our young listeners the importance of developing Christian values.

Spiritbuilding Bible Challenge CDs

- Over 4,000 questions covering the Old and New Testaments
- For use in Bible classes, lesson reviews, suppplemental class work, Bible labs, homeschooling and gaming

Spiritbuilding Publishing